MW01028020

SQUASH LVERS
COOK BOOK

GOLDEN WEST ☼ PUBLISHERS

Front cover photo of summer squash: "Squash Medley" courtesy Syngenta Seeds/ROGERS Brand. Variety from top to bottom: Gentry (yellow crookneck), Spineless Beauty (medium green zucchini), Golden Delight (yellow zucchini), Sunburst (yellow scallop), Starship (green scallop) and Noche (dark green zucchini)

Back cover photo: "Squash Collage" courtesy Rupp Seeds, Inc. Varieties are: The four green, white and orange striped squash are Festival (winter squash). The two blue squash are Blue Majic (winter hubbard). The two orange ones are Orange Dawn (winter buttercup) and the two tan ones are Pilgrim (winter butternut).

Acknowledgments

Winter Comfort Veggie Soup and *Sweet Tater Challenge* recipes courtesy Roger Rupp, Rupp Seeds Inc. http://www.ruppseeds.com.

The following are excerpted from Golden West Publishers cookbooks:

Escabeche, Golden Squash Muffins, Zesty Zucchini Pancakes, Squash & Green Chile Molds and *Crookneck Squash Soup* recipes from Lynn Nusom *(Billy the Kid Cookbook, Christmas in Arizona, Christmas in New Mexico).*

Calabacitas and *Zucchini Casserole* recipes from Mari Meyers *(Gourmet Gringo).*

Fresh Squash Salsa and *Zucchini Cake* recipes from Susan Bollin *(Salsa Lovers Cook Book, Sedona Cook Book).*

Calabacitas con Crema, Mixed Sausage and Squash Grill, Land of Enchantment Spice Mix, Hot Cilantro Lime Oil and *Anasazi Squash* recipes from Sandy Szwarc *(Real New Mexico Chile).*

Call 800-658-5830 for complete cookbook catalog.

Printed in the United States of America

ISBN #1-885590-94-6

Copyright © 2003 by Golden West Publishers. All rights reserved. This book or any portion thereof, may not be reproduced in any form, except for review purposes, without the written permission of the publisher.

Information in this book is deemed to be authentic and accurate by author and publisher. However, they disclaim any liability incurred in connection with the use of information appearing in this book.

Golden West Publishers, Inc.

4113 N. Longview Ave.
Phoenix, AZ 85014, USA
(800) 658-5830

Visit our website: goldenwestpublishers.com

Table of Contents

Table of Contents (continued)
Side Dishes

Breads & Desserts

Introduction

Squash is one of nature's finest gifts to man! While squash has been a staple item in the Americas for more than 5,000 years, it has attained great significance in our modern-day diets because it is tasty, versatile and nutritious.

When the Pilgrims came to America, pumpkins and squash were shared by the Native Americans and these items became part of our everyday American culture. Other explorers returned from their journeys throughout the Americas with still more varieties of squash, in varying shapes, sizes and colors.

Squash are divided into two types, summer and winter. Summer squash have thinner rinds, are more delicate and taste best when harvested in the early stages of growth. Winter squash are harvested at a mature stage, when their shells have grown hard and inedible. While both have similar growing seasons, winter squash are so named because they can be stored longer, often throughout the winter months.

Summer squash have lighter colored flesh and contain a much higher water content. They are low in calories (about 19 per cup of raw sliced squash), offer a moderate amount of nutrients and are generally inexpensive.

Winter squash have darker flesh that is more nutritious, richer in complex carbohydrates and, in many cases, beta-carotene. Whereas summer squash can be eaten raw or cooked, winter squash are almost always cooked. Most types of winter squash are interchangeable in these recipes. The same holds true for the summer squash.

All winter squash contain significant quantities of key antioxidants, especially Vitamin C and carotenoids, as well as folate, calcium and other minerals, including magnesium and potassium. Carotenoids have been shown to be helpful in protecting against various types of cancer.

Squash Tips & Techniques

Winter Squash

Choose a winter squash that is heavy for its weight and has a deep, even color. Squash without cuts, bruises and blemishes and with a few inches of stem will last longer. Some varieties, such as banana squash, are sold in the supermarkets already cut into large pieces: look for deep-colored flesh.

Winter squash usually have very tough rinds and can be difficult to cut. Since quite a few recipes in this book call for cutting a squash in half before cooking, here are some tips on cutting winter squash (we strongly advise letting the adult in your household cut the winter squash!) First, make sure to wash the squash before cutting to avoid spreading bacteria.

Using a heavy chef's knife, place the blade of the knife along the length of the squash. Use a hammer or mallet to drive the knife into the squash until it breaks in half. Another method is to insert the point of a heavy chef's knife vertically into the squash and pull the knife down while twisting left to right.

If the squash is particularly difficult to cut, you can pierce the skin with a few holes, bake it at 350° for about 20 minutes, then remove it and cut.

Summer squash

Choose summer squash that have a heavy feel, an even color and no cuts or bruises. Summer squash are best when harvested before they grow too large and the skin begins to harden. Choose small squash for most recipes. Use summer squash over 10 inches long grated in breads and relishes. Don't use summer squash over 12 inches long.

Summer squash have a delicate flavor that can be easily covered up by overseasoning, so go lightly on the spices. Our favorites include dill, parsley, rosemary, cumin, savory, oregano and basil.

Appetizers

Zucchini Squares

These can be prepared ahead of time and refrigerated. Serve them at your next get-together and you'll be the hit of the party!

1 cup BISQUICK®
4-5 med. ZUCCHINI, thinly sliced or grated
1/2 cup VEGETABLE or OLIVE OIL
4 EGGS, lightly beaten
1/2 cup chopped ONION
1/2 cup grated PARMESAN CHEESE
1 clove GARLIC, chopped
2 Tbsp. PARSLEY
1/2 tsp. SALT
1/2 tsp. OREGANO
Freshly ground BLACK PEPPER to taste

Preheat oven to 350°. In a mixing bowl, combine all ingredients and blend well. Spread mixture in a greased 13 x 9 baking pan. Bake for 30 minutes, until top is golden brown. Make sure mixture is set in the middle before removing from oven. Cool for 15 minutes; cut into 1-inch squares and serve.

Stuffed Zucchini Cups

These are a tasty addition to any party menu!

3 med. (6-inch) ZUCCHINI, cut into 2-inch rounds

Gently scoop out core of zucchini rounds, leaving 1/4-inch on the bottom of each "cup". Place cups on a baking sheet. Spoon **Crab-Swiss Stuffing** or **Chicken Curry Stuffing** into zucchini cups. Bake at 375° for 15 minutes.

Crab-Swiss Stuffing

ZUCCHINI PULP
2 cans (7.5 oz. ea.) CRABMEAT, drained and flaked
3 GREEN ONIONS, thinly sliced
1 cup MAYONNAISE
2 tsp. LEMON JUICE
1/2 tsp. CURRY POWDER
2 cups grated SWISS CHEESE
1 can (8 oz.) WATER CHESTNUTS, drained and diced

In a bowl, combine zucchini pulp, crabmeat, onion, mayonnaise, lemon juice and curry powder. Stir in 1 1/2 cups of the Swiss cheese and the water chestnuts. After cups have been filled, sprinkle tops with remaining Swiss cheese and garnish with paprika.

Chicken Curry Stuffing

1 1/2 Tbsp. OLIVE OIL
1 sm. ONION, chopped
2 1/2 Tbsp. FLOUR
2 Tbsp. CURRY POWDER
1/4 cup CHICKEN STOCK
1 cup SOUR CREAM
1 Tbsp. SUGAR or HONEY
1/4 cup grated CARROT
SALT and PEPPER to taste
2 Tbsp. LEMON JUICE
2 cups cooked and shredded CHICKEN
ZUCCHINI PULP

In a skillet, heat oil and sauté onion until translucent. Stir in flour and curry powder and cook for 1 minute. Stir in chicken stock and sour cream. Add remaining ingredients and simmer for an additional 10 minutes.

Escabèche

This is a delightful way to serve vegetables as an appetizer or first course. Vegetables such as carrots, cauliflower and zucchini are cooked with spices and then marinated with lime juice and hot chiles. This is great served with crisp homemade tortilla chips and a cool drink or Mexican beer.

1 WHITE ONION, chopped
12 cloves GARLIC, sliced
4 CARROTS, thinly sliced
    on the diagonal
1/2 tsp. coarsely ground
    BLACK PEPPER
1 1/2 cups WHITE VINEGAR
1/2 cup OLIVE OIL
2 cups WATER
2 Tbsp. SALT
6 BAY LEAVES, broken in half

1 head CAULIFLOWER, broken
    into flowerettes
3 ZUCCHINI, sliced
    on the diagonal
1 tsp. ground THYME
1 tsp. ground OREGANO
1 tsp. ground MARJORAM
1/2 cup LIME JUICE
1 JICAMA, peeled and sliced
1/2 cup PICKLED JALAPEÑOS

In a large nonreactive pot, combine all the ingredients, except for the lime juice, jicama and jalapeños. Bring to a boil; reduce heat and simmer for 10 minutes; let cool. Add lime juice, jicama and jalapeños. Store, covered, in refrigerator for up to 2 weeks. Remove bay leaves before serving.

Zucchini Dip

1 cup SOUR CREAM
2 pkgs. (3 oz. ea.) CREAM CHEESE WITH CHIVES
2 cups grated and drained ZUCCHINI
1 tsp. dried SWEET BASIL

In a medium bowl, blend sour cream and cream cheese together. Stir in zucchini and basil. Chill.

Makes about 3 cups.

Vegetable Pancakes with Pesto Cream

These tasty pancakes make a great hors d'ouvre!

2 lg. POTATOES, shredded
3 med. CARROTS, shredded
2 med. ZUCCHINI, shredded
3/4 cup chopped GREEN ONIONS
1 tsp. SALT
3/4 cup FLOUR
3 EGGS, beaten
1/4 tsp. PEPPER
1 Tbsp. VEGETABLE OIL

Rinse and drain shredded potatoes; squeeze out excess moisture with paper towels and place in a large bowl. Add carrots, zucchini, onions and salt. Let stand for 10-15 minutes or until vegetables release some liquid. Stir in flour, eggs and pepper. In a large skillet, heat oil. Pour 1/4 cup of batter for each pancake into skillet and flatten slightly with a spatula. Cook pancakes until golden brown and crispy on both sides. Serve with ***Pesto Cream.***

Pesto Cream

1 cup SOUR CREAM   2 Tbsp. BASIL PESTO

In a small bowl, combine sour cream and pesto together and stir until smooth.

Zucchini Fritters

2 lbs. ZUCCHINI, grated
1 cup FLOUR
2 EGGS
2 Tbsp. grated ONION
1 can (7 oz.) diced GREEN CHILES
VEGETABLE OIL

In a large bowl, combine zucchini, flour, eggs, onion and green chiles and mix well. In a skillet, heat vegetable oil and carefully drop in batter by tablespoon. Cook until browned and crispy. Drain well on paper towels.

Salads

Ensalada de Calabacitas

(Zucchini Salad)

1 lb. ZUCCHINI, sliced into 1/8-inch thick rounds
2 POBLANO CHILES, roasted, seeded and peeled,
   cut into thin strips
1 cup cooked or canned CORN
1/2 cup finely chopped WHITE ONION
1 Tbsp. finely chopped fresh EPAZOTE LEAVES
SALT and PEPPER
1/4 cup OLIVE OIL
2 Tbsp. WINE VINEGAR

In a saucepan, cook zucchini rounds in water just until crisp-tender; set aside to cool. Combine zucchini with chile strips and corn. In a shallow dish, layer zucchini mixture with onion and epazote. Add salt and pepper to taste. Mix oil and vinegar together and pour over top. Let sit at room temperature for 1 hour to absorb flavors.

Six-Layer Salad

1 pkg. (16 oz.) MACARONI SHELLS
1/2 cup sliced GREEN ONIONS, with tops
1/4 cup cooked and crumbled BACON
1 cup MAYONNAISE
1/4 cup LEMON JUICE
3 Tbsp. grated PARMESAN CHEESE
1 tsp. SUGAR
1/2 tsp. GARLIC POWDER
4 cups bite-size pieces of SALAD GREENS
2 ZUCCHINI, sliced
1 cup sliced CAULIFLOWER
1 cup BROCCOLI FLOWERETS
2 med. TOMATOES, cut into wedges
SALAD DRESSING

Cook macaroni according to package directions; drain. Rinse with cold water and drain again. In a medium bowl, combine macaroni, onions and 2 tablespoons of the bacon. In another bowl, mix mayonnaise, lemon juice, Parmesan cheese, sugar and garlic powder together and then stir into macaroni mixture. In a 3 1/2-quart salad bowl, layer salad greens, macaroni mixture, zucchini, cauliflower, broccoli and tomatoes. Pour your favorite salad dressing evenly over the top. Cover and refrigerate at least 2 hours. Sprinkle with remaining bacon just before serving.

Garden Dressing

1 cup YELLOW SQUASH
2 cups WATER
5 Tbsp. TAMARI
1 tsp. PARSLEY
5 Tbsp. PEANUT BUTTER

2 Tbsp. LEMON JUICE
1/2 ONION
2 cloves GARLIC
6 Tbsp. VEGETABLE OIL
1 tsp. BASIL

Cut squash in large chunks. Combine all ingredients in a blender and blend until smooth. Chill and serve.

Grilled Vegetable Salad

1 ZUCCHINI
2 YELLOW SQUASH
1 lg. ONION
1 EGGPLANT
OLIVE OIL

Dressing:
    1 RED CHILE PEPPER, roasted and diced
    Dash of COARSE SALT
    Dash of RED PEPPER FLAKES
    Dash of freshly ground BLACK PEPPER
    1/2 tsp. chopped fresh PARSLEY
    1/2 tsp. OREGANO
    1 clove GARLIC, minced
    2 tsp. BALSAMIC VINEGAR
    2 Tbsp. EXTRA VIRGIN OLIVE OIL

Slice zucchini and squash lengthwise into 1/4-inch thick slices. Peel and slice onion into 1/4-inch thick slices. Peel and slice eggplant lengthwise into 1/2-inch thick slices. Rub all vegetables with olive oil to coat. Grill approximately 4 minutes per side or until just soft. Remove from grill, dice and place in a salad bowl. In a small bowl, combine seasonings with garlic, vinegar and oil. Pour dressing over vegetables and toss to mix. Let sit at least 20 minutes to blend flavors. Serve at room temperature.

Growing Squash

Winter and summer squash are planted in the spring after all danger of frost is past. Winter squash grows all summer and is always harvested at the mature stage in early autumn before the first frost. Summer squash are harvested throughout the summer and fall. They should be picked when they are small and tender.

Peppy Pasta & Bean Salad

1/2 lb. ROTINI PASTA
2 Tbsp. OIL
1 RED BELL PEPPER, sliced into strips
1/4 cup chopped RED ONION
2 ZUCCHINI, thinly sliced
2 cloves GARLIC, minced
3/4 tsp. ITALIAN SEASONING
1 can (15 oz.) KIDNEY BEANS, drained

Dressing:
   1/3 cup OIL
   2 Tbsp. minced fresh PARSLEY
   JUICE of 1 LEMON
   3/4 tsp. HOT PEPPER SAUCE
   SALT and PEPPER to taste

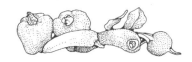

Cook pasta according to package directions; drain. In a large skillet, heat 2 tablespoons oil and sauté bell pepper, onion, zucchini, garlic and Italian seasoning until crisp-tender; set aside to cool. In a large bowl, toss pasta, beans and vegetables together. Chill for several hours. Just before serving, whisk together dressing ingredients. Pour dressing over pasta, bean and vegetable mixture and toss to coat well.

Garden Salad

1/2 head RED LETTUCE
1/2 head BUTTER LETTUCE
1/4 head ROMAINE LETTUCE
2 ZUCCHINI, diced
1 leaf KALE, chopped
2 cloves GARLIC, finely minced

1 cup ALFALFA SPROUTS
1 leaf SWISS CHARD, chopped
1 cup SPINACH, chopped
1 AVOCADO, peeled and sliced
1 RED ONION, thinly sliced
SALAD DRESSING

Tear all lettuce into bite-size pieces. In a salad bowl, combine all ingredients and toss well. Add your favorite dressing.

Pasta Salad

1 pkg. (12 oz.) ROTELLE, or other curly pasta
1 ZUCCHINI, sliced and cut into half moons
1 YELLOW SQUASH, sliced and cut into half moons
1 sm. bunch BROCCOLI, cut into flowerets
1/2 cup diced CHEDDAR CHEESE
1/2 cup diced PEPPER JACK CHEESE
1/2 pkg. (1-2 oz.) sliced SALAMI
1 Tbsp. dried PARSLEY
BOTTLED ITALIAN DRESSING
PARMESAN CHEESE
SALT and freshly ground BLACK PEPPER

Prepare pasta according to package directions. While pasta is cooking, steam vegetables until crisp-tender. In a large bowl, combine pasta, vegetables, cheddar and pepper jack cheeses, salami and parsley. Pour desired amount of dressing over salad and liberally sprinkle with Parmesan cheese. Add salt and pepper to taste.

Zucchini Salad

3 CARROTS, shredded
6 ZUCCHINI, shredded
1/2 ONION, diced
1/2 GREEN BELL PEPPER, diced
1 clove GARLIC, minced

Dressing:
1/2 tsp. THYME   2 Tbsp. VINEGAR
1/2 tsp. CHERVIL   1/2 tsp. BASIL
Dash of PEPPER   1/8 tsp. DRY MUSTARD
1/2 cup WATER

In a salad bowl, combine vegetables and garlic and toss. Place dressing ingredients in a blender and blend for 3-4 seconds. Pour over vegetables and refrigerate for 2 hours. Garnish with **TOMATO WEDGES** when serving.

Curlicue Pasta Salad

This is a tangy, refreshing salad. The homemade marinade is worth the extra effort.

1 pkg. (16 oz.) TRI-COLORED ROTINI PASTA

Marinade:

1 3/4 cups OIL	1 1/2 tsp. SALT
2/3 cup WHITE WINE VINEGAR	1/2 tsp. PEPPER
2 Tbsp. LEMON JUICE	1/2 tsp. dried OREGANO
1 Tbsp. DIJON MUSTARD	1/4 tsp. SUGAR
2 cloves GARLIC, minced	

1 1/2 cups sliced MUSHROOMS
1 1/2 cups sliced ZUCCHINI
1 1/2 cups sliced RED OR GREEN BELL PEPPER
1/2 cup finely chopped fresh PARSLEY
1/2 cup chopped GREEN ONIONS, with tops

Cook pasta according to package directions; drain. Place pasta in a large salad bowl. In a bowl, whisk the marinade ingredients together. Pour over warm pasta and mix well. Stir in remaining ingredients. Cover and refrigerate for 6 hours or overnight. Stir before serving.

What's the Difference
Between Winter Squash and Summer Squash?

Winter squash are late growing, less symmetrical with a hard rind and tend to be rough, warty or oddly shaped. They are harvested later than summer squash and earned their name because they can be stored all winter long. Summer squash are small, fast growing and usually consumed before the seeds and rinds begin to harden. Their flesh is more delicate in flavor and texture than winter squash.

Power Garden Salad

This salad is designed for health and energy.

1/2 head ROMAINE LETTUCE, torn into pieces
2 cups fresh SPINACH LEAVES, torn into pieces
2 YELLOW CROOKNECK SQUASH, diced
1 CARROT, diced
1/2 cup diced RED CABBAGE
2 lg. RADISHES, sliced
1/4 cup sliced RED ONION
2 GREEN ONIONS, chopped
1/2 RED DELICIOUS APPLE, chopped
1/4 RED BELL PEPPER, chopped
1/4 GREEN BELL PEPPER, chopped
1 stalk CELERY, diced
1/4 cup ALFALFA SPROUTS
1/2 cup frozen PEAS, thawed
1/4 cup RAISINS
1/4 cup FETA CHEESE
SALAD DRESSING of choice

In a large salad bowl, combine all ingredients and toss well. Cover and chill before serving. Serve with salad dressing.

Too Many Squash?

An abundance of summer squash recipes probably came about because summer squash plants produce abundant yields. It is common for a family that grows summer squash to offer their extra squash to their neighbors, but chances are the neighbors will be trying to give away their own!

Types of Squash

Summer Squash

Zucchini (Open pollinated):
 Black Zucchini
 Black Beauty
 Cocozelle
 Vegetable Marrow White
  Bush
Zucchini (hybrid):
 Aristocrat
 Chefini
 Classic
 Elite
 Embassy
 President
 Spineless Beauty
Golden Zucchini (hybrid)
 Gold Rush
Yellow Crookneck
 Early Yellow Summer Crook-
  neck
 Sundance
Yellow Straightneck
 Early Prolific Straightneck
 Goldbar
Scallop
 White Bush Scallop
 Peter Pan
 Scallopini
 Sunburst

Other Summer Squash
 Butter Blossom
 Gourmet Globe
 Sun Drops

Winter Squash

Acorn
 Cream of the Crop
 Ebony
 Swan White

Table Ace
Table Gold
Table King
Table Queen
Tay-Belle
Delicata
 Delicata
 Honey Boat
 Sugar Loaf
 Sweet Dumpling
Spaghetti
 Orangetti
 Pasta
 Stripetti
 Tivoli
 Vegetable Spaghetti
Butternut
 Butterbush
 Early Butternut
 Ponca
 Puritan
 Supreme
 Ultra
 Waltham
 Zenith
All Season
Banana
Buttercup
Delicious
Emerald Bush Buttercup
Honey Delight
Gold Nuggett
Baby, Blue, Chicago, Green
 Golden and Warted
 Hubbard
Mooregold
Sweet Mama
Sweet Meat
Red Kuri

Soups & Stews

Crookneck Squash Soup

2 Tbsp. OLIVE OIL
1/4 cup BUTTER
1 lg. ONION, chopped
2 stalks CELERY, chopped
3 YELLOW CROOKNECK SQUASH, sliced
2 CARROTS, sliced
1 GREEN BELL PEPPER, chopped
2 SWEET POTATOES, peeled and cubed
2 WHITE POTATOES, peeled and cubed
2 mild GREEN CHILES, roasted, peeled,
    seeded and chopped
1 tsp. freshly ground BLACK PEPPER
1/4 tsp. CAYENNE
1 tsp. SALT
2 cups CHICKEN BROTH or STOCK
6 cups WATER
Sprigs of CILANTRO

Heat oil and butter in a large soup pot and sauté onion, celery and squash for 5-6 minutes. Add the remaining ingredients except cilantro and cook, covered, for 1 hour. Spoon into individual soup bowls. Garnish with sprigs of cilantro and serve.

Serves 6-8.

Microwave Pumpkin Soup

1 (8 lb.) PUMPKIN, cut in half,
    seeds and pulp removed
1/3 cup finely chopped ONION
1/4 cup BUTTER
3 cups HOT WATER
2 Tbsp. INSTANT CHICKEN
    BOUILLON GRANULES

1/4 tsp. NUTMEG
1/8 tsp. WHITE PEPPER
1/8 tsp. GINGER
1/8 tsp. ALLSPICE
1 stick CINNAMON
1/2 cup HALF and HALF

Place half of the pumpkin in an 8 x 8 baking dish and cover with plastic wrap. Microwave at High for 10-15 minutes or until tender, rotating dish every 5 minutes. Repeat with remaining half. Spoon pumpkin from shells. Mash or process in a food processor until smooth. Set aside. Place onion and butter in a 5-quart casserole and cover. Microwave at High, stirring once, for 3-5 minutes or until onion is tender. Mix in mashed pumpkin and remaining ingredients and return to microwave, uncovered. Reduce power to Medium and heat, for 8 to 10 minutes or until flavors have blended, stirring 2 or 3 times. Spoon into 2 freezer containers (may be frozen for up to 2 months.) When ready to use, place contents of one container in a 1 1/2-quart casserole and microwave at Medium for 15-20 minutes, breaking up and stirring 2 or 3 times.

Each container of soup serves 4-6.

Note: Microwave and freeze for up to 2 months.)

Pumpkins and Squash

Pumpkins are from the horticultural family, Cucurbitaceae, *along with squashes, melons, cucumbers and gourds. Of the 700 species, some are raised for fruits, while others are used for decorative ornaments, utensils and even sponges.*

Butternut Squash Soup

1 BUTTERNUT SQUASH	3 Tbsp. BUTTER
NONSTICK VEGETABLE OIL SPRAY	3 cups CHICKEN BROTH
	1-2 cups WATER
1 Tbsp. freshly grated GINGER	SOUR CREAM for garnish
1 cup chopped ONION	

Preheat oven to 350°. Cut squash in half lengthwise and scoop out seeds. Spray a roasting pan with vegetable oil and arrange the halves, cut-side-down, in the pan. Bake squash for 40-45 minutes or until very tender. Set aside to cool. When squash is completely cool, scoop the flesh from the skin. Place ginger, onion and butter in a saucepan; sauté until onion is translucent. Add broth to pan, cover and simmer for 10 minutes. Mix in squash pulp. Transfer mixture, in batches, to blender or food processor and purée until smooth, adding enough water to achieve desired consistency. Return soup to saucepan and heat. When serving, garnish each portion with a dollop of sour cream.

Serves 4.

Spinach-Zucchini Soup

2 tsp. MARGARINE	1 1/2 Tbsp. fresh BASIL
1 cup diced ONION	Dash of SALT
2 ZUCCHINI, cubed	Dash of PEPPER
2 cups VEGETABLE STOCK	1 Tbsp. LEMON JUICE
1 bunch SPINACH	

In a soup pot, heat margarine and sauté onions and zucchini until onions are translucent. Stir in stock and bring to a boil. Add spinach, basil, salt and pepper. Cover pot and cook for 5 minutes. Purée soup in blender, return to pot and simmer for 5 minutes. Stir in lemon juice.

Serves 2-4.

Yellow Squash Bisque

Soup Base:

3 Tbsp. MARGARINE	1 CHICKEN BOUILLON CUBE
1 lg. ONION, chopped	1/4 cup DRY SHERRY
4 YELLOW SQUASH, chopped	1 tsp. dried BASIL
1 1/2 cups WATER	1/2 tsp. dried THYME

2/3 cup INSTANT MILK POWDER
1/3 cup COOL WATER
4 Tbsp. SOUR CREAM
1/4 cup chopped fresh CHIVES
Freshly ground BLACK PEPPER

In a large saucepan, melt margarine and sauté onions until translucent. Add yellow squash and cook until tender. Stir in water, bouillon cube, sherry, basil and thyme. Cover pan and simmer for 15 minutes. Remove from heat and let soup base cool to room temperature. Pureé soup base in a blender until smooth. Mix milk powder with cool water until dissolved, then stir into soup base. Pour entire mixture back into saucepan and cook over medium heat for 10 minutes. Spoon into soup bowls and garnish with sour cream, chives and pepper to taste.

Serves 3-4.

About Summer Squash

Summer squash, high in vitamins A and C as well as niacin, have thin, edible skins and soft seeds. Their tender flesh has a high water content, a mild flavor and doesn't require long cooking. The most widely available varieties of summer squash are crookneck, zucchini, yellow and pattypan. Select smaller squash with bright-colored skin and no spots or bruises. Summer squash is very perishable and should be refrigerated in a plastic bag for no more than 5 days. It can be prepared by a variety of methods including steaming, baking, sautéing and deep-frying.

Hearty Soup

1/4 cup BUTTER or MARGARINE
1 lg. ONION, chopped
3 med. SWEET POTATOES, peeled and chopped
3 ZUCCHINI, chopped
1 bunch BROCCOLI, chopped
2 qts. CHICKEN BROTH
2 med. POTATOES, peeled and shredded
2 tsp. CELERY SEED
2 tsp. CUMIN
1 tsp. PEPPER
2 cups LIGHT CREAM

In a large kettle, melt butter and sauté onion until translucent. Add sweet potatoes, zucchini and broccoli and sauté for 5 minutes. Stir in broth and simmer for an additional 5 minutes. Add potatoes and seasonings and continue to cook for 10 minutes until vegetables are tender. Stir in cream and heat through.

Serves 6-8.

Vegetable Soup Supreme

1 ONION
1/2 cup GREEN BEANS
2 CARROTS
2 YELLOW CROOKNECK SQUASH
4 TOMATOES
1 Tbsp. PARSLEY
1 POTATO
1/2 sm. peeled EGGPLANT

2 stalks CELERY
2 stalks BOK CHOY
1/2 cup MUSHROOMS
1 Tbsp. VEGETABLE OIL
8 cups VEGETABLE STOCK
1 tsp. BASIL
1 tsp. SALT

Dice all vegetables. In a large saucepan, heat oil, add vegetables and sauté until just tender. Add vegetable stock and seasonings. Simmer for 50 minutes.

Serves 6-8.

Winter Comfort Veggie Soup

1 lb. SWEET ITALIAN SAUSAGE
4 cups CHICKEN BROTH
2 cups shredded CABBAGE
1 lg. ONION, diced
1 lg. PARSNIP, diced
1/2 cup diced RED BELL PEPPER
1 cup diced CARROTS
1 cup diced CELERY
1 FENNEL BULB, finely sliced
1 cup diced BUTTERNUT SQUASH
PARMESAN or ASIAGO CHEESE, optional

In a skillet, crumble and then fry sausage; set aside. Place chicken broth in a saucepan; add shredded cabbage and onion. When cabbage and onion are just tender, add remaining vegetables and the sausage. Cook until vegetables are tender. Sprinkle each serving with cheese as desired.

Albondigas

(Meatball Soup)

1 lb. LEAN GROUND ROUND
  STEAK
6 GREEN ONIONS, diced
1 tsp. GARLIC PEPPER
1/2 tsp. crushed dried RED
  CHILE PEPPERS
1/2 tsp. ground ALLSPICE

3 cans (10 oz. ea.) BEEF
  CONSOMMÉ
2 med. TOMATOES, diced
2 ZUCCHINI, diced
1 cup thinly sliced CABBAGE
1 cup fresh or frozen CORN

In a mixing bowl, combine ground steak, onions, garlic pepper, red peppers and allspice. Form mixture into balls about 1 inch in diameter. Place consommé in a Dutch oven and heat to boiling. Gently add meatballs, one at a time, to the boiling consommé. Add tomatoes, zucchini, cabbage and corn. Reduce heat and simmer gently, uncovered, for 45 minutes.

Beef Stew
in a "Pumpkin Pot"

1 lb. BEEF CUBES	2-3 POTATOES, diced
2 tsp. OIL	1/2 lb. CARROTS, sliced
1 tsp. PEPPER	1 cup GREEN BEANS
6 cups HOT WATER	1 cup LIMA BEAMS
3 Tbsp. CORNSTARCH	1 cup CORN
1/2 cup COLD WATER	1 stalk CELERY, chopped
1 sm. PUMPKIN	1 ONION, chopped
1/2 tsp. SALT	

In a large saucepan, heat oil; add beef cubes and cook until well-browned on all sides; sprinkle with pepper. Add hot water; cover and simmer for 3 hours. Mix cornstarch with cold water and stir into beef broth. Cut off the top of the pumpkin and scrape out seeds; sprinkle interior with salt. Parboil potatoes for 10-15 minutes and steam carrots for 15 minutes. Add meat and vegetables to pumpkin and place lid on top. Bake at 375° for 1 1/2-2 hours or until pumpkin is tender. When serving, be sure to scoop flesh from inside of pumpkin.

Serves 4-6.

Sweet Pumpkin Soup

2 cups PUMPKIN, pared and diced	6 tsp. BUTTER
2 cups WATER	1/2 tsp. SALT
3 tsp. SUGAR	3 cups MILK

Put pumpkin, water, sugar, 3 teaspoons of the butter and salt in a saucepan. Bring to a boil and cook for 15 minutes or until pumpkin is soft. Rub through a sieve, add milk and bring back to a boil. Add remaining butter. Sprinkle top with croutons when serving.

Serves 4-6.

Caldo de Pollo

(Chicken Soup)

Chicken soup is not only good for your soul, but good for your body, too!

4 skinless CHICKEN BREASTS
8 cups WATER
2 ANAHEIM or NEW MEXICO CHILES, seeded and diced*
1 ONION, quartered
4 stalks CELERY, diced into large pieces
4 CARROTS, sliced into large pieces
1 BAY LEAF
1/2 tsp. GARLIC SALT
1/2 tsp. CAYENNE
1/2 cup chopped fresh CILANTRO
1/2 tsp. CUMIN
2 ZUCCHINI, sliced into large pieces
SALT and PEPPER

In a large pot, cover chicken breasts with water and bring to a boil. Cook for 10 minutes; skim off excess fat that rises to the surface. Add chiles, onions, celery, carrots, bay leaf and seasonings. Reduce heat; cover pot and simmer for 30 minutes. Remove chicken, debone, then stir back into the soup. Add zucchini and salt and pepper to taste. Continue simmering until vegetables are tender. Remove bay leaf before serving.

Serves 8.

*Note: Be sure to wear rubber gloves and do not touch your face when seeding and dicing chiles.

Don't Have It? Don't Worry!

With only slight variations in taste and texture, the different summer squash varieties can be substituted for each other in these recipes.

Mixed Vegetable Stew

3 cloves GARLIC, minced
1 Tbsp. SESAME SEEDS
1 EGGPLANT, peeled and
    diced
3 Tbsp. VEGETABLE OIL
2 cups VEGETABLE JUICE
3 CARROTS, diced

1 ZUCCHINI, sliced
1 YELLOW SQUASH, sliced
1 PATTYPAN SQUASH, chopped
12 fresh MUSHROOMS, sliced
1/2 cup TOMATO SAUCE
1/2 tsp. OREGANO
1/4 tsp. MARJORAM

In a saucepan, sauté garlic, sesame seeds and eggplant in vegetable oil for 4 minutes. Add juice, carrots and squash and continue cooking for 4 minutes. Add mushrooms, tomato sauce and seasonings. Reduce heat and simmer for 12 minutes. Serve over couscous, rice or pasta.

Serves 4-6.

Summertime Stew

1 (3/4 lb.) boneless, skinless WHOLE CHICKEN
    BREAST, chopped
4 cups CHICKEN STOCK
2/3 cup chopped ONION
1 clove GARLIC, crushed
2 ZUCCHINI, chopped
2 PATTYPAN SQUASH, chopped
2 TOMATOES, seeded and chopped
1 1/2 cups fresh or frozen CORN
1 can (4 oz.) diced GREEN CHILES
3 Tbsp. chopped fresh CILANTRO LEAVES
1 tsp. CUMIN
1 tsp. dried OREGANO
SALT and PEPPER to taste

Place all ingredients in a large pot and stir. Simmer, covered, over medium-low heat for 1 hour or until vegetables are tender.

Serves 4.

Fruity Zucchini Stew

2 Tbsp. SALAD OIL
2 lbs. BEEF STEW MEAT, cubed
2 med. ONIONS, quartered
1 tsp. SALT
1/8 tsp. PEPPER
6 whole ALLSPICE
1 BAY LEAF
1 BEEF BOUILLON CUBE

2 1/2 cups WATER
3 CARROTS, cut in strips
1 lb. ZUCCHINI, thinly sliced
1 cup DRIED APRICOTS
1/2 tsp. SUGAR
1 tsp. FLOUR
1/4 cup WATER
SALT and PEPPER

In a Dutch oven or large saucepan, heat oil and cook beef until browned on all sides. Add onions, seasonings, bouillon cube and water and bring to a boil. Reduce heat, cover and simmer for 1 hour, or until meat is tender. Add carrots and cook for an additional 5 minutes. Add zucchini, apricots and sugar. Continue cooking for 10 minutes or until vegetables are tender. Remove bay leaf and discard. Blend flour with 1/4 cup water until smooth and gradually stir into stew. Cook, stirring constantly, until sauce thickens and boils for 1 minute. Add salt and pepper to taste.

Serves 4-6.

Hopi Corn Stew

2 tsp. LARD
1 cup finely chopped BEEF or GOAT
2 cups chopped SUMMER SQUASH
2 cups GREEN CORN, shelled from cob
1 Tbsp. FLOUR
1/4 cup WATER
SALT

In skillet, heat lard and cook meat until brown. Add squash, corn and water to cover. When squash is tender, stir in flour that has been made into a paste with the water. Add salt to taste. Stir well and cook for an additional 5 minutes.

Serves 2-4.

Main Dishes

Stuffed Acorn Squash

2 ACORN SQUASH
1/2 cup uncooked BROWN RICE
1 lb. MAPLE-FLAVORED PORK SAUSAGE
1 EGG
1 can (2.5 oz.) sliced MUSHROOMS, drained
SALT to taste

Preheat oven to 350°. Cut each squash in half lengthwise; discard seeds. Place squash halves, cut-side-down in a 12 x 8 baking dish. Bake for 45 minutes. Prepare rice according to package directions. In a large skillet, cook sausage until brown; drain and place in a bowl. Mix sausage with egg, mushrooms and rice. Turn squash halves cut-side-up in baking dish and sprinkle with salt. Spoon sausage mixture into squash halves. Cover with foil, return to oven and bake for an additional 15 minutes or until tender. Serve immediately.

Serves 4.

Anasazi Squash Salad

The Southwestern pueblo Indians are believed to be descendants of the Anasazi, or "ancient ones." This main dish salad brings the fresh tastes of their native summer squashes into modern times.

2 YELLOW SQUASH or ZUCCHINI
SALT
1 cup diced CHICKEN or TURKEY BREAST
2 tsp. LAND OF ENCHANTMENT® SPICE MIX
1 Tbsp. OLIVE OIL
1/3 cup chopped MARINATED SUNDRIED TOMATOES, patted dry
1/2 cup chopped GREEN ONIONS
1/4 cup chopped, roasted and peeled NEW MEXICO
    GREEN CHILES
1/3 cup chopped fresh CILANTRO LEAVES
2 Tbsp. LIME JUICE
2 Tbsp. TEQUILA
1 cup grated mild GOAT CHEESE or any WHITE CHEESE

Coarsely grate squash into a colander and sprinkle lightly with salt. Drain for 30 minutes, then squeeze dry; set aside. In a bowl, toss chicken with **Land of Enchantment Spice Mix** Heat oil in a large skillet over medium-high heat. Add chicken and cook, stirring occasionally, until golden. Stir in squash, tomatoes, green onions and chile. Stir gently while cooking over medium heat for 8 minutes or until zucchini is crisp-tender. Add remaining ingredients and toss. Heat thoroughly.

Serves 4.

Land of Enchantment Spice Mix

2 Tbsp. SALT	1 1/2 tsp. DRIED OREGANO
1 Tbsp. GREEN CHILE POWDER	1/2 tsp. CHILE CARIBE
2 tsp. NEW MEXICO RED CHILE POWDER	2 tsp. GRANULATED GARLIC
	2 tsp. GRANULATED ONION
1 tsp. GROUND CUMIN	

Toss all together and store in an airtight container.

Tetrazzini Zucchini

4 cups diced ZUCCHINI
1/2 tsp. SALT
1/2 tsp. PEPPER
1/3 cup BUTTER
2 1/4 cups diced cooked HAM
1 cup sliced MUSHROOMS
1/2 cup chopped ONION
1/3 cup FLOUR

1 cup HOT CHICKEN STOCK
1 1/4 cups MILK
2/3 cup shredded SWISS
    CHEESE
1/2 tsp. DRY MUSTARD
1/2 cup grated PARMESAN
    CHEESE

Steam zucchini until crisp-tender; drain and sprinkle with salt
and pepper. In a large skillet, melt butter and sauté ham and
mushrooms; remove with slotted spoon and set aside. Add
onions to skillet and sauté until golden. Sprinkle in flour and
gently blend. Allow flour to cook slightly, then gradually stir in
hot chicken stock and milk. Simmer, stirring continuously,
until sauce thickens. Add Swiss cheese and mustard and
continue stirring until cheese melts. Add ham, mushrooms and
zucchini. Pour into a buttered casserole dish; sprinkle top with
Parmesan cheese. Broil until bubbly.

Serves 6.

A Zucchini by Any Other Name

*The word zucchini comes from the Italian
"zucchino" meaning a small squash. The term
squash comes from the Indian "skutasquash"
meaning "green thing eaten green." The French
term for zucchini is "courgette," and this term is
often used for yellow squash as well.*

Chiles Stuffed with Squash Blossoms

Squash blossoms are a very popular filling for poblano chiles. This filling is lighter than most, so if you are serving this for dinner, a rice or pasta dish is a good accompaniment.

Since both squash blossoms and poblano chiles reach the height of their growing season at the same time, summer gardeners will find this a fun way to use the squash blossoms, and a bit different from most of the other recipes for these flowers.

3 cups SQUASH BLOSSOMS
2 Tbsp. VEGETABLE OIL
1 med. ONION, finely chopped
1 clove GARLIC, finely chopped
1 sm. TOMATO, finely chopped
SALT
6 lg. POBLANO CHILES, roasted, peeled and seeded
1/4 cup FLOUR
BASIC EGG COATING (see next page)
OIL for cooking
Grated QUESO AÑEJO or any hard, grating cheese

Remove prickly centers and stems from squash blossoms. Thoroughly rinse squash blossoms; drain in colander. In a large skillet, heat oil and sauté onion and garlic until onion is translucent. Add tomatoes and squash blossoms and cook, covered, over low heat for 5 minutes. Remove lid and continue cooking until tomato liquid has evaporated. Add salt to taste. Remove mixture from heat and allow to cool. Slit chiles lengthwise and stuff, dividing mixture evenly between them. Pat dry and lightly coat with flour. Just before cooking, prepare **Basic Egg Coating** mixture. Gently roll chiles in egg mixture and coat evenly. Cook in hot oil until golden brown on each side; remove and drain. Serve with grated cheese sprinkled on top.

Serves 3. (Continued next page)

Chiles Stuffed with Squash Blossoms
(continued from previous page)

Basic Egg Coating

3 EGGS, separated and at room temperature
1/4 tsp. SALT

In a small bowl, beat egg whites until stiff peaks form. In a separate bowl, lightly beat egg yolks and salt together; fold gently into the egg whites.

Note: Although preparation of chiles and filling can be done in advance, the ***Basic Egg Coating*** must be used immediately after it is made to avoid becoming runny. Once the chiles have been fried, they can be drained and reheated later.

Surf 'n' Turf Kabob

1/2 lb. SHRIMP, peeled
1 lb. BEEF SIRLOIN STEAK, cut into 1-inch pieces
2 ZUCCHINI, cut diagonally into 1-inch pieces
2 ears CORN, cut into 1-inch pieces
2 sm. ONIONS, cut into wedges
1 GREEN BELL PEPPER, cut into 1-inch pieces
Cooked RICE

Alternate all kabob ingredients on skewers. Grill or broil kabobs, turning and brushing with ***Lemon Basting Sauce,*** until meat reaches desired doneness.

Lemon Basting Sauce

1/4 cup WATER
1/2 cup KETCHUP
1/4 cup finely chopped ONION
1 Tbsp. BROWN SUGAR
3 Tbsp. LEMON JUICE

2 Tbsp. COOKING OIL
2 tsp. MUSTARD
2 tsp. WORCESTERSHIRE SAUCE
1/2 tsp. CHILI POWDER

In a small saucepan, combine all sauce ingredients and simmer, uncovered, for 10 minutes, stirring occasionally.

Mexican Flag Chiles

The green and red of the chiles with the white of the crema
(sour cream), achieve the "Mexican flag" effect.

Filling:
   2 Tbsp. OLIVE OIL
   4 GREEN ONIONS, tops included, finely chopped
   1 cup 1/4-inch cubed ZUCCHINI
   3 cups CORN, fresh or frozen
   1 sprig EPAZOTE
   1/2 cup finely chopped fresh CILANTRO LEAVES
   SALT and PEPPER

4 med. RED POBLANO CHILES, roasted, peeled and seeded
4 med. GREEN POBLANO CHILES, roasted, peeled and seeded

Garnish:
   1 cup SOUR CREAM
   1 lg. WHITE ONION, cut into 8 thin slices
   1 lg. TOMATO, cut into 8 slices

In a large skillet, heat oil and sauté green onions for 2 minutes. Add zucchini, corn and epazote and sauté for an additional 5 minutes, or until vegetables are crisp-tender. Stir in cilantro leaves and salt and pepper to taste and mix well. Allow filling to cool to room temperature; remove epazote sprig. Slit chiles lengthwise and stuff, dividing mixture evenly between them. If serving hot, lightly sauté chiles in a nonstick pan in a small amount of olive oil, turning gently to heat each side. Arrange one red and one green chile side by side on each serving plate. Spoon 1/4 cup sour cream down the middle so that some covers each chile. Garnish with onion and tomato slices.

Serves 4.

Note: The epazote sprig called for above, provides this recipe with its unique Mexican taste. It is also known as "Mexican tea" and is often used in black bean recipes, as it seems to help negate the gaseous effects of the beans.

Turkey-Rice Casserole

2 cups cooked WHITE or BROWN RICE
2 cups cooked, cubed TURKEY
2 ZUCCHINI, cut into 1/4-inch rounds
3/4 cups shredded MONTEREYJACK CHEESE
1 can (4 oz.) GREEN CHILES, chopped and drained
2 med. TOMATOES, halved lengthwise, then sliced crosswise

Topping:

1 cup SOUR CREAM	PEPPER
1/3 cup chopped ONION	3/4 cup shredded MONTEREY
1/2 tsp. SALT	JACK
1/4 tsp. OREGANO	

Spread rice in a greased 2-quart baking dish. Top with layers of turkey, zucchini, cheese, green chiles and tomatoes. Mix all topping ingredients together, except for the cheese and spread over casserole; sprinkle with cheese. Bake at 350° for 30 minutes.

Serves 6.

Mostaccioli Primavera

3 cups uncooked MOSTACCIOLI	3 GREEN ONIONS, sliced
4 Tbsp. SUNFLOWER OIL	1 1/2 cups diced TOMATOES
1 RED BELL PEPPER, julienned	2 Tbsp. chopped fresh CHIVES
2 CARROTS, julienned	2 Tbsp. chopped fresh DILL
2 ZUCCHINI, julienned	SALT and PEPPER
2/3 cup fresh ORIENTAL PEA	1/4 cup toasted SUNFLOWER
PODS, cut in halves	SEEDS

Prepare mostaccioli according to package directions; drain. In a large nonstick skillet, heat oil and sauté red bell pepper and carrots for 6 minutes. Add zucchini, pea pods and green onions and sauté for 5 minutes. Stir in tomatoes, chives and dill. Season with salt and pepper to taste. Heat until warmed through, then toss the vegetable mixture with the mostaccioli. Sprinkle with sunflower seeds.

Serves 6.

Zucchini-Stuffed
Chicken Breasts

4 ZUCCHINI
1/4 tsp. SALT
4 Tbsp. BUTTER
1 med. ONION, chopped
2 EGG YOLKS, beaten
24 oz. SMALL-CURD COTTAGE CHEESE
1/2 tsp. BASIL, crushed
2 Tbsp. grated PARMESAN CHEESE
12 deboned CHICKEN BREAST HALVES, with skin

Coarsely grate zucchini into a colander and sprinkle lightly with salt. Drain for 30 minutes and squeeze dry. In a large skillet, melt 2 tablespoons butter and sauté onion and zucchini until onion is translucent. Add all remaining ingredients, except chicken. Cook just until flavors combine, stirring occasionally. Stuff 1/4 cup of filling under the skin of each chicken breast. Arrange chicken in a buttered baking dish and dot with remaining butter. Bake at 350° for 30-35 minutes or until golden brown.

Serves 12.

Zucchini Bake

1 lg. (10-inch) ZUCCHINI
1 lb. GROUND BEEF
1/4 tsp. SALT
1/4 tsp. PEPPER
1 EGG
10 SODA CRACKERS, crushed
1/4 lb. CHEESE, shredded

Cut zucchini lengthwise, remove seeds and set aside. In a bowl, mix ground beef, salt, pepper, egg and crackers. Stir in zucchini seeds. Spoon mixture into zucchini shells. Bake at 400° for 1 hour. Just before serving, sprinkle cheese on top and bake an additional 10-15 minutes or until cheese is melted.

Serves 6.

Zucchini Lasagna

1 lb. ITALIAN SAUSAGE
1/2 cup chopped ONION
1 can (15 oz.) TOMATO SAUCE
1/2 cup WATER
1/4 tsp. SALT
1/4 tsp. OREGANO
3/4 cup grated PARMESAN CHEESE
2 Tbsp. FLOUR
6 LASAGNA NOODLES, cooked and drained
2 cups sliced ZUCCHINI
12 oz. grated MOZZARELLA CHEESE

In a large skillet, brown sausage and onion together; drain excess fat. Stir in tomato sauce, water, salt and oregano. Simmer for 30 minutes, stirring occasionally. In a small bowl, combine Parmesan cheese with flour. Grease a 13 x 9 baking dish and place 3 lasagna noodles on the bottom. Top with half of the zucchini, half of the Parmesan mixture, half of the meat sauce and half of the mozzarella cheese. Repeat layer, except for the mozzarella cheese and end with top layer of noodles. Bake at 375° for 20-25 minutes or until zucchini is tender. Top with remaining mozzarella cheese and return to oven until cheese melts. Let stand 10 minutes before serving.

Serves 8.

Leading Squash Producers

Florida, California and Georgia lead the nation in production of squash. In 2001, the value of Florida's squash crop was $48.4 million, while the value of the total U.S. crop was $183 million.

Zucchini & Meatballs

1 tsp. INSTANT BEEF BOUILLON
1/2 cup WATER
2 slices BREAD, crumbled
2 tsp. chopped fresh PARSLEY
1 lb. GROUND BEEF or VEAL
1 Tbsp. OIL
1 med. ONION, chopped

1 clove GARLIC, minced
1/2 tsp. SALT
1 tsp. grated CHEDDAR
  CHEESE
1 can (8 oz.) TOMATO SAUCE
4 ZUCCHINI, cut
  into 1/4-inch slices

In a large bowl, dissolve bouillon in water. Add bread, parsley and meat and mix well. Shape into 16 meatballs; refrigerate until firm. In a skillet, heat oil and sauté onion and garlic until onion is translucent; remove with a slotted spoon. Add meatballs to skillet and cook until brown on all sides; remove and set aside. In a separate skillet, place meatballs, onion, garlic and remaining ingredients and bring to a boil. Reduce heat, cover and simmer for 10 minutes or until zucchini is tender.

Serves 4.

Skillet Chicken & Rice

2 whole boneless CHICKEN BREASTS, skinned and sliced
1/2 lb. ZUCCHINI, thinly sliced
1 1/2-2 cups BROCCOLI FLOWERETS
1/2 cup chopped GREEN ONION
1 can (14.5 oz.) DICED TOMATOES, undrained
3 cups cooked WHITE or BROWN RICE
1/4 cup chopped fresh PARSLEY
1/2 tsp. SALT
1/4 tsp. PEPPER
Pinch of dried OREGANO

Coat large skillet with cooking spray. Sauté chicken until lightly browned. Add zucchini and broccoli and cook until crisp-tender. Stir in remaining ingredients. Cover, reduce heat and simmer for 15 minutes or until heated through.

Serves 8-10.

Vegan Sauté

1/2 sq. TOFU, cubed
1 cup sliced ZUCCHINI
1 Tbsp. OIL
1 cup chopped MUSHROOMS
1 ONION, chopped
1/3 cup CHICKPEAS (garbanzo beans)
1/3 cup chopped ROMAINE, RED SWISS CHARD or SPINACH
Miso broth:
   1/2 cup WATER
   1/2 Tbsp. MISO
   1 tsp. chopped fresh GINGER
   1 tsp. MARGARINE
SALT and PEPPER
Cooked LONG-GRAIN BROWN RICE

Steam tofu and zucchini. In a large skillet, heat oil and sauté mushrooms, onion, chickpeas and romaine until tender. Add tofu and zucchini to skillet. In a small bowl, blend ingredients for miso broth and add to skillet. Reduce heat. Stir in margarine and season with salt and pepper to taste. Serve over rice.

Serves 2.

Venison-Zucchini Dinner

2 cloves GARLIC, thinly sliced
1 (1 1/2-inch thick) VENISON
   STEAK
Dash of PEPPER
4 BACON SLICES

1/2 cup diced ONION
2 ZUCCHINI, sliced
1 cup sliced fresh
   MUSHROOMS

Place slices of garlic on steak and sprinkle with pepper. Wrap steak with bacon slices and brown in a large skillet. Add onion, zucchini and mushrooms. Cook until vegetables are soft and steak is done.

Serves 4.

Turkey Casserole

1 lb. GROUND TURKEY
1/4 cup chopped ONION
1 can (15 oz.) TOMATO SAUCE
1 Tbsp. GARLIC SALT
1 tsp. dried BASIL LEAVES
1 tsp. dried OREGANO LEAVES
1 lb. SUMMER SQUASH, cut into 1/4-inch strips
1/2 cup grated ROMANO CHEESE
1 1/2 cups LOW FAT COTTAGE CHEESE
1 EGG
2 Tbsp. FLOUR
1 cup shredded MOZZARELLA CHEESE

In a large skillet, cook turkey and onion until meat is brown; drain excess liquid. Add tomato sauce and spices and bring to a boil. Simmer over low heat for 10 minutes. In a bowl, mix squash with Romano cheese, cottage cheese and egg. Prepare a 9 x 9 baking pan with cooking spray. In the baking pan, layer 1/2 of the squash, a sprinkle of flour, 1/2 of the cottage cheese mixture and 1/2 of the meat sauce. Top with 1/2 of the mozzarella cheese. Repeat with remaining ingredients. Bake, uncovered, at 350° for 45 minutes. Let stand for 10 minutes before serving.

Serves 4.

Shelf Life of Summer Squash

Because summer squash are harvested before they develop a hard rind, they have a shorter shelf life than winter squash...only a few days. Store them dry in the crisper drawer of the refrigerator. Moisture leads to early decay, so only wash summer squash just before preparation.

Stuffed Green Peppers

4 lg. GREEN BELL PEPPERS
1 cup RICE
3 med. TOMATOES, diced
1 ZUCCHINI, diced
8 oz. frozen MIXED VEGETABLES, cooked and drained
1 med. ONION, diced
1 1/2 tsp. GARLIC POWDER
2 tsp. DILL WEED
1 Tbsp. BASIL
SALT and PEPPER to taste
1 Tbsp. JANE'S® CRAZY SALT
1 lb. GROUND TURKEY, cooked, drained

Remove tops, core and seed bell peppers; set aside. Cook rice according to package directions. In a large bowl, combine remaining ingredients with rice and stir well. Spoon mixture into each pepper. For best flavor, refrigerate overnight. Bake at 375° for 45 minutes.

Serves 4.

Zucchini Pie

1 lb. LEAN GROUND BEEF
1/2 cup chopped GREEN BELL PEPPER
1/2 cup chopped ONION
1 tsp. ea. PARSLEY, GARLIC SALT, OREGANO
1 can (15 oz.) TOMATOES
4 cups chopped ZUCCHINI
SALT and PEPPER to taste
1/2 cup grated CHEDDAR CHEESE
1/2 cup grated PARMESAN CHEESE
1/2 cup DRY BREAD CRUMBS
2 (9-inch) unbaked PIE SHELLS

In a large skillet, brown beef with bell pepper, onion and seasonings. Add tomatoes, zucchini, salt and pepper. Cook for 5 minutes. Stir in cheddar cheese, Parmesan cheese and bread crumbs and mix well. Pour into pie shell; top with second crust and vent. Bake at 350° for 30-45 minutes or until crust is golden.

Serves 4-6.

Stuffed Zucchini Rings

1 lg. ZUCCHINI, cut crosswise into 1 1/2-inch thick slices
1 cup cooked RICE
1/2 cup shredded CHEDDAR CHEESE
1/2 cup minced ONION
1/2 tsp. GARLIC POWDER
1/2 tsp. SEASONED SALT
1/2 tsp. PEPPER
1/2 cup minced HAM, BEEF or CHICKEN
Dash of PAPRIKA
1/3 cup RED WINE

Scoop out cores of zucchini rings and place the rings on a greased baking sheet. In a large bowl, thoroughly combine zucchini pulp and remaining ingredients, except paprika and wine. Spoon stuffing into rings; garnish with paprika. Spoon a teaspoon of wine onto each ring. Bake at 375° for 20 minutes or until zucchini is tender. Spoon remaining wine over rings and bake for an additional 15 minutes. Remove with spatula.

Serves 6.

Calabacitas con Jamon

(Squash with Ham)

3 Tbsp. SALAD OIL
1 sm. ONION, sliced
1 med. GREEN BELL PEPPER, cut into strips
1 sm. PIMENTO, cut into strips
2 lg. fresh TOMATOES, coarsely chopped
2 cups cooked YELLOW SQUASH
4 cups cooked HAM, cut into strips
1/2 tsp. SALT
1/4 tsp. PEPPER
1/8 tsp. GARLIC POWDER
2 tsp. PARSLEY FLAKES

In a skillet, heat oil and sauté onions. Add bell pepper and pimento and cook for 4-5 minutes. Stir in remaining ingredients and blend well. Cover and simmer for 15 minutes or until vegetables are tender.

Serves 4-6.

No-Pasta Lasagna

1 lb. GROUND BEEF
2 Tbsp. BUTTER
2 cloves GARLIC, minced
1/2 tsp. THYME
1/2 tsp. OREGANO
1/2 tsp. SEASONING SALT
2 Tbsp. FLOUR
1 1/2 cups TOMATO JUICE

SALT and PEPPER
4 ZUCCHINI
1 cup shredded MOZZARELLA
   CHEESE
1/2 cup crushed POTATO CHIPS
1/2 cup shredded CHEDDAR
   CHEESE

In a large skillet, cook beef; drain and set aside. In the same skillet, melt butter and sauté garlic, thyme, oregano and seasoning salt for 2 minutes, stirring continuously. Blend in flour; add tomato juice and cook to thicken. Add salt and pepper to taste. Slice zucchini lengthwise into 1/4-inch slices and layer in a greased 13 x 9 pan; add a layer of the meat and then a layer of mozzarella cheese. Repeat layers. Pour sauce over top. Cover with foil and bake at 350° for 45 minutes. Remove foil; top with potato chips and cheddar cheese. Return to oven and bake for an additional 10 minutes.

Serves 4.

Bubble & Squeak

This Welsh recipe is delicious!

3 POTATOES, unpeeled
4 cups chopped CABBAGE,
   blanched
1/2 med. ONION, chopped
2 ZUCCHINI, grated

1/4 cup chopped HAM
PEPPER to taste
3 slices BACON, cooked
   and crumbled, drippings
   reserved

In a saucepan, boil potatoes until tender; drain. Slightly mash potatoes and combine with remaining ingredients, except for drippings. In a non-stick skillet, heat bacon drippings; press potato mixture into skillet. Cook over medium heat for 30 minutes or until golden brown; do not stir. Invert onto a plate and serve.

Serves 4-6.

Baked Spaghetti Squash with Garden Sauce

1 SPAGHETTI SQUASH
2 Tbsp. OLIVE OIL
3/4 cup peeled and finely chopped EGGPLANT
2 CARROTS, finely chopped
1 med. ONION, finely chopped
1 GREEN BELL PEPPER, finely chopped
1-2 cloves GARLIC, minced
3 Tbsp. chopped fresh BASIL
3 Tbsp. chopped fresh OREGANO
1 1/2 cups chopped TOMATOES
1 can (15 oz.) TOMATO SAUCE
Dash of SALT

Split squash in half; remove seeds and place cut-side-down in a shallow pan filled with 1 inch of water. Bake squash at 400° for 30 minutes. In a large skillet, heat oil and sauté eggplant, carrots, onion, bell pepper and garlic until just tender. Add basil and oregano and continue cooking for 3-5 minutes. Stir in tomatoes, tomato sauce and salt and bring to a boil. Serve over baked spaghetti squash.

Serves 4.

About Winter Squash

Winter squash can be baked, steamed or simmered. They are a good source of iron, riboflavin and vitamins A and C. Winter squash have hard, thick skins and seeds. The flesh is firmer than that of summer squash and therefore requires longer cooking. Winter squash varieties include acorn, buttercup, hubbard, spaghetti and turban. Winter squash is best from early fall through the winter. Choose squash that are heavy for their size and have a hard, deep-colored rind free of blemishes. Depending on the variety, they can be kept in a cool, dark place for a month or so.

Zucchini-Mushroom Casserole

1 1/2 lbs. GROUND BEEF
1 GREEN BELL PEPPER, diced
1 med. ONION choppedF
1 tsp. OREGANO
1/2 tsp. GARLIC POWDER
3 ZUCCHINI, cubed
1 cup INSTANT RICE
1 can (4 oz.) MUSHROOMS, with liquid
1 can (10.75 oz.) CREAM OF MUSHROOM SOUP
1 cup grated CHEDDAR CHEESE

Sauce:
   1 can (10.75 oz.) CREAM OF MUSHROOM SOUP
   1/2 cup liquid from ZUCCHINI
   1 can (4 oz.) MUSHROOMS, with liquid

In a large skillet, combine ground beef, bell pepper, onion, oregano and garlic powder and cook until meat is brown; set aside. In a saucepan, cover zucchini with water and boil for 3 minutes; drain, reserve liquid and set aside. In a bowl, combine beef mixture, rice, mushrooms and soup and mix well. In a casserole dish, layer 1/3 of beef mixture then 1/2 of the zucchini. Repeat layers; top with beef mixture. Sprinkle cheddar cheese over all. Bake at 350° for 30 minutes. In a saucepan, combine ingredients for sauce and heat until warm. Pour over casserole.

Serves 4-6.

Zucchini Fairies?

In some parts of the country, people are warned to look out for "zucchini fairies" (gardeners who leave baskets of squash on neighbors' doorsteps!) It seems they appear in the middle of the night to "dispose" of their excess crops!

Chicken-Zucchini Casserole

3-5 sm. ZUCCHINI, cut into chunks
1 sm. ONION, chopped
1 cup SOUR CREAM
1 can (10.75 oz.) CREAM OF CHICKEN SOUP
1/2 cup MARGARINE, melted
1 pkg. (6 oz.) CHICKEN FLAVOR STOVE TOP® STUFFING MIX
2 cups diced cooked CHICKEN
SALT and PEPPER

In a large saucepan, cover zucchini and onion with water. Boil for 5 minutes; drain well. Stir in sour cream and soup; set aside. Toss margarine with stuffing and combine 3/4 of stuffing with zucchini mixture. Add chicken and salt and pepper to taste. Spoon mixture into casserole dish; sprinkle remaining stuffing over the top. Bake at 350° for 45 minutes.

Serves 4.

Venison & Squash

2 Tbsp. OLIVE OIL
2 lbs. POTATOES, thinly sliced
2 cloves GARLIC, minced
1 lb. VENISON, sliced thin
1 ONION, chopped
1 GREEN BELL PEPPER, chopped
2 YELLOW SQUASH, sliced
SALT and PEPPER to taste
KALE or COLLARD GREENS, washed

Heat oil in a large skillet over medium-high heat and cook potatoes and garlic for 10 minutes, stirring occasionally. Stir in remaining ingredients, except kale. Cook for 15 minutes, stirring frequently, until meat is browned and vegetables are tender. Top with kale and cook, covered, for 2 minutes or until kale is wilted.

Serves 4.

Mixed Sausage and Squash Grill

2 ZUCCHINI, cut into 1-inch slices
2 YELLOW SQUASH, cut into 1-inch slices
1/2 lg. RED ONION, cut into 1-inch pieces
1 RED or YELLOW BELL PEPPER, seeded and
     cut into 1-inch pieces
1 lb. asstd. SAUSAGES (Bratwurst, Italian, Kielbasa, Linguisa),
     cut into 1-inch pieces
3/4 cup HOT CILANTRO LIME OIL
4 cups CHICKEN STOCK
1 1/3 cups uncooked RICE
SALT and PEPPER

Alternately skewer zucchini, yellow squash, onion, bell pepper and sausage on metal skewers. These may be made several hours ahead, covered tightly in plastic wrap and refrigerated. Start grill, bringing coals to medium heat. Place kabobs approximately 6 inches above heat. Grill, brushing generously with *Hot Cilantro Lime Oil*, for 15-20 minutes or until vegetables are tender and golden brown. Meanwhile, in a large saucepan, bring chicken stock to a boil and stir in rice. Add salt and pepper to taste. Reduce heat, cover and simmer for 15-20 minutes or until liquid is absorbed and rice is tender; fluff rice with a fork. To serve, place rice on serving plates and top with grilled kabobs. Drizzle extra *Hot Cilantro Lime Oil* on top.

Serves 4.

Hot Cilantro Lime Oil

1/4 cup LIME JUICE
1/3 cup + 1 Tbsp. OLIVE OIL
2 Tbsp. LAND OF ENCHANTMENT SPICE MIX (See page 30)
1/4 cup chopped fresh CILANTRO LEAVES

In a small bowl, whisk all the ingredients together.

Vegetable Fajitas

2 ZUCCHINI, julienned
2 YELLOW SQUASH, julienned
2 GREEN BELL PEPPER,
   cut into strips

1 ONION, cut into wedges
1 TOMATO, cut into wedges
2 Tbsp. OIL

Place vegetables in a shallow glass baking dish or a locking plastic bag. Pour **Fajita Marinade** over vegetables and refrigerate for 2 hours. In a large skillet, heat oil and add vegetables; sauté until desired tenderness. Serve with warmed **FLOUR** or **CORN TORTILLAS.** Accompany with plenty of **shredded LETTUCE, chopped TOMATOES, SOUR CREAM, SALSA** and **REFRIED BEANS.**

Fajita Marinade

1/2 cup WATER
1/4 cup LEMON JUICE
2 cloves GARLIC, crushed
1 Tbsp. WORCESTERSHIRE SAUCE
1/2 tsp. OREGANO

1/2 tsp. CUMIN
2 tsp. BROWN SUGAR
Dash of TABASCO®
1/8 tsp. LIQUID SMOKE

In a glass bowl, combine all ingredients and blend well.

Serves 4.

Did You Know?

While pumpkins and winter squash have been popular in the United States since the time of the Pilgrims, zucchini has only been popular for the last forty or fifty years!

Turkey-Zucchini Dinner

2 Tbsp. OIL
1 Tbsp. BUTTER
4 TURKEY DRUMSTICKS
1 med. ONION, sliced
1 can (16 oz.) STEWED
　TOMATOES
3 CHICKEN BOUILLON CUBES
1/2 tsp. SALT
1/2 tsp. GARLIC SALT

1/2 tsp. OREGANO
1/2 tsp. BASIL LEAVES,
　crumbled
8 sm. or 4 lg. POTATOES
3 ZUCCHINI, cut into 3/4-inch
　thick slices
1 Tbsp. CORNSTARCH
2 Tbsp. COLD WATER

In a large skillet, heat oil and melt butter. Add drumsticks and brown on all sides. Place drumsticks in large baking pan, top with onion slices; set aside. In the same skillet, heat tomatoes with chicken bouillon and seasonings and pour over drumsticks. Cover pan with foil, crimp edge to seal. Bake at 325° for 2 hours until almost tender, basting once or twice. Boil potatoes, cool slightly and remove skins. Tuck potatoes and zucchini in and around drumsticks and spoon liquid over them. Cover and bake for an additional 30 minutes. Mix cornstarch and water and stir into hot sauce. Bake for 5-10 minutes to thicken slightly. Arrange drumsticks and vegetables on a hot platter and serve.

Serves 8.

Bass Fillets Supreme

2 Tbsp. BUTTER
6 MUSHROOMS, sliced
1 ONION, sliced
2 ZUCCHINI, sliced
2 CARROTS, chopped
2 ripe TOMATOES, chopped

2 tsp. chopped CHIVES
2 tsp. BASIL
1 clove GARLIC, crushed
SALT and BLACK PEPPER
4 BASS fillets

In a skillet, melt butter and sauté mushrooms for 3-5 minutes. Add onion, zucchini, carrot, tomatoes, herbs, garlic and salt and pepper to taste. Simmer for 10 minutes. Place fillets in a buttered baking dish and cover with sauce. Bake at 350° for 20-30 minutes.

Serves 4-6.

Acorn Squash
with Beef & Potatoes

1 ACORN SQUASH, peeled, seeded and cut into 1-inch pieces
2 lbs. LEAN BEEF, cut into 1 1/2-inch cubes
2 lg. RED POTATOES, cut into 1 1/2-inch pieces
1 lg. ONION, halved and sliced
1 pkg. (.875 oz.) MUSHROOM GRAVY MIX
1 can (14.5 oz.) diced TOMATOES, with juice
1/4 tsp. ALLSPICE
1/4 tsp. GARLIC POWDER
1/4 tsp. PEPPER
2 BAY LEAVES
1/2 tsp. SALT

Combine all ingredients in a slow cooker. Cover and cook on Low for 8-10 hours. Remove bay leaves before serving.

Serves 6-8.

Broiled Ahi

(Yellow Fin Tuna)

1 lb. AHI
1 Tbsp. CANOLA OIL
1/2 tsp. PAPRIKA
COOKING SPRAY
2 LEMONS
1 Tbsp. OLIVE OIL

6 CARROTS, peeled and
    julienned
1 lg. ZUCCHINI, peeled and
    julienned
BLACK PEPPER

Clean fish and discard all outer dark skin. Mix canola oil with paprika and brush over fish. Place fish in a 10 x 9 baking dish that has been prepared with cooking spray. Broil for 5 minutes on each side. Squeeze lemon juice onto fish while it is broiling. In a skillet, heat olive oil and stir-fry carrots and zucchini for 5-8 minutes. Add pepper to taste. Serve with fish.

Serves 4.

 # Acorn Squash Substitutions

The following squash varieties can be substituted for acorn squash: buttercup (a little drier), butternut (nuttier flavor), banana (larger), Hubbard (larger). Even pumpkins can be used in place of acorn squash.

Winter Squash

Acorn squash: *Popular because of their taste and size. Rind is very hard.*

Banana squash: *Often found already cut into chunks at supermarkets. Flesh is beautiful golden color.*

Buttercup squash: *Flesh is sweet and creamy, but it tends to be a little dry.*

Butternut squash: *Popular variety that is very easy to use. Rind is thinner than other winter varieties. Flavor is sweet, moist and nutty.*

Sweet potato squash *(Bohemian squash): Has creamy pulp that tastes like sweet potatoes.*

Golden nugget squash *(Oriental pumpkin): Pleasant flavor; not as much flesh. Hard rind.*

Hubbard squash: *Tasty flesh; hard rind; difficult to cut.*

Kabocha squash *(Japanese squash): Orange flesh that is sweeter, drier, less fibrous and tastes like sweet potatoes.*

Pumpkin: *Use the small sugar pumpkin for baking.*

Spaghetti squash: *After it is cooked the flesh resembles long yellow strands of spaghetti. Great substitute for pasta.*

Sweet dumpling squash: *Flesh is sweeter and drier than other winter squash; peel is softer and can even be eaten.*

Turban squash: *Often better used as a centerpiece or as a soup tureen.*

Side Dishes

Nutty Squash

2 ACORN or BUTTERNUT SQUASH
VEGETABLE OIL

Split acorn squash lengthwise and remove seeds. Place squash cut-side-down on an oiled baking pan. Bake at 350° for 30 minutes. Fill squash with *Walnut Filling.* Cover with foil and bake at 350° for 25 minutes.

Walnut Filling

3-4 Tbsp. BUTTER
Dash of SALT
1/2 cup chopped ONION
1 clove GARLIC, minced
1 stalk CELERY, chopped
1/4 cup chopped WALNUTS
1/4 cup SUNFLOWER SEEDS
SALT and PEPPER

1/2 tsp. RUBBED SAGE
1/2 tsp. THYME
1 cup coarsely crumbled
**   WHOLE-WHEAT BREAD**
JUICE of 1/2 LEMON
1/4 cup RAISINS, optional
1/2 cup grated CHEDDAR
**   CHEESE**

In a skillet, heat butter and salt. Sauté onion, garlic, celery, walnuts and sunflower seeds. Cook over low heat until onion is translucent, nuts are browned and celery is tender. Season with salt and pepper to taste. Add remaining ingredients, except for the cheese. Cook over low heat, stirring frequently, for 5-8 minutes. Remove from heat and mix in cheese.

Serves 8.

Baked Squash Casserole

2 lbs. YELLOW SQUASH, sliced
1 stick MARGARINE, melted
2 EGGS, beaten
2 Tbsp. MILK
2 Tbsp. dried MINCED ONION
1 tsp. SALT
PEPPER to taste
2 cups RITZ® CRACKER CRUMBS, 1/2 cup reserved for topping
1 1/2 cups grated CHEDDAR CHEESE, 1/2 cup reserved for
    topping

In a saucepan, cover squash with water and cook until tender; drain and mash. Stir in the remaining ingredients and mix well. Pour into a large greased baking dish. Sprinkle with reserved cracker crumbs and cheddar cheese. Bake at 375° for 45 minutes.

Serves 8.

Zesty Zucchini Cakes

2 EGGS, separated
1/2 cup ALL-PURPOSE FLOUR
1/2 tsp. SALT
1/4 tsp. BLACK PEPPER
2 Tbsp. chopped GREEN CHILES (fresh or canned)
2 cups shredded ZUCCHINI
OIL for frying

In a mixing bowl, beat egg yolks and combine with flour, salt and pepper. Stir in green chile and zucchini. Beat egg whites until stiff. Fold into zucchini mixture. In a large skillet, heat 1 inch of oil and carefully drop in zucchini mixture by tablespoons. When edges turn golden brown, flip cakes and cook until both sides are golden brown.

Serves 4.

Marinated Vegetables

1 cup SNOW PEAS
1 cup chopped BROCCOLI
1 cup diced CARROTS
1 cup diced ZUCCHINI
1 cup cooked LIMA BEANS

Marinade:

1/3 cup CANOLA OIL
3 Tbsp. LEMON JUICE
1/8 tsp. BLACK PEPPER
1 Tbsp. TAMARI

1 tsp. BASIL
1 tsp. ONION POWDER
1/4 tsp. DILL WEED

Steam snow peas, broccoli, carrots and zucchini until soft. Add lima beans and then transfer mixture to a salad bowl. In a separate bowl, combine marinade ingredients; pour over vegetables and beans; cover and chill for at least 2 hours.

Serves 4-6.

No-Bake Tofu Quiche

This quick and easy quiche contains no dairy products.

1 lb. FIRM TOFU, rinsed and drained
1 pkg. (10 oz.) FIRM SILKEN TOFU
1 Tbsp. TAMARI or SOY SAUCE
1/2 tsp. SEA SALT
4 Tbsp. CASHEW NUT BUTTER
1 clove GARLIC, minced
2 oz. fresh PARSLEY, minced
2 Tbsp. WHOLE-WHEAT BREAD CRUMBS
2 ZUCCHINI, sliced
4 oz. MUSHROOMS, sliced

Combine first 8 ingredients in a food processor or blender and process until well-blended. Arrange zucchini in an 8-inch pie plate and top with mushrooms. Spoon tofu mixture evenly over vegetables. Chill until firm.

Serves 4.

Corn & Zucchini Pudding

4 Tbsp. BUTTER or MARGARINE
1/2 cup chopped ONION
1 can (15 oz.) CREAM STYLE CORN
1 can (15.25 oz.) WHOLE KERNEL CORN, drained
    (or 2 cups fresh)
4 sm. ZUCCHINI, cut into 1/4-inch thick rounds
GARLIC POWDER
2 EGGS, beaten
1 cup MILK or 1/2 cup MILK and 1/2 cup HEAVY CREAM
1/8 tsp. freshly grated NUTMEG
SALT and PEPPER to taste
1 cup grated CHEDDAR CHEESE
1/3 cup grated PARMESAN CHEESE

Preheat oven to 375°. In a skillet, melt butter and sauté onion until translucent. Stir in corn and zucchini and cook until zucchini is slightly tender; sprinkle with garlic powder to taste. Remove skillet from heat and blend in eggs, milk, nutmeg, salt and pepper. Stir in cheddar cheese and Parmesan cheese. Pour mixture into a 5-cup baking dish. Bake for 30 minutes or until set in center and top edges are golden.

Serves 6-8.

Orange Acorn Squash

3 ACORN SQUASH
6 Tbsp. BROWN SUGAR
3 Tbsp. BUTTER

1 Tbsp. grated ORANGE PEEL
3 med. ORANGES, peeled
    and sectioned

Cut squash in half lengthwise and remove seeds. Place cut-side-down in a shallow baking pan. Bake at 375° for 40 minutes. Turn cut-side-up and add remaining ingredients, divided evenly between all. Continue baking until squash is tender (approximately 20 minutes), basting with melted butter and juice from bottom of pan.

Serves 6.

Zucchini Quiche

Crust:

1/4 cup CORNMEAL
1/4 cup FLOUR
1/2 tsp. SALT
2 Tbsp. BUTTER

1/4 cup VEGETABLE
SHORTENING
2 Tbsp. COLD WATER

Filling:

4 EGGS
1 cup HEAVY CREAM
SALT and PEPPER to taste
1 sm. ONION, chopped
1/2 cup CORN

1/2 cup GREEN BEANS
1/2 cup chopped ZUCCHINI
1/2 cup shredded SHARP
CHEDDAR CHEESE

For the crust: In a large bowl, combine cornmeal, flour and salt. Cut in butter and shortening using a fork or pastry blender until mixture resembles a coarse meal. Add water and mix until dough forms a ball. Refrigerate dough on waxed paper for at least 1/2 hour. Turn chilled dough out onto a floured surface. Using a rolling pin, roll dough into a large circle. Transfer to a 9-inch pie pan and bake in a preheated 350° oven for 5 minutes. For the filling: In a large bowl, beat eggs, cream, salt and pepper. Stir in onion, corn, beans and zucchini. Add cheddar cheese and stir again. Pour quiche mixture into pie shell. Return to oven and bake for 10 minutes at 425°. Reduce temperature to 350° and continue baking for an additional 30 minutes or until quiche is almost set in the center. Let quiche stand for 15 minutes before slicing.

Serves 4-6.

Historic Origins

Zucchini has been a popular item in Central and South America for several thousand years, but the zucchini we enjoy today is a variety of summer squash developed in Italy.

Squash & Green Chile Molds

3 Tbsp. BUTTER
1/3 cup BREAD CRUMBS
1 cup CREAM or MILK
1/2 tsp. SALT
1/2 tsp. ground BLACK PEPPER
1/2 tsp. GARLIC POWDER

1/2 tsp. ground CUMIN
3 EGGS, separated
1 1/2 cups cooked, chopped
    YELLOW SQUASH
1/2 cup chopped GREEN
    CHILE

In a large saucepan, melt butter and lightly brown bread crumbs. Add cream, salt, pepper, garlic powder and cumin. Cook over low heat, stirring constantly, until mixture is smooth. Remove from heat and let mixture cool slightly. In a bowl, beat egg yolks and add cream mixture, a little at a time, beating constantly. Pour mixture back into saucepan and cook for 3-4 minutes, stirring well. Remove from heat and stir in squash and chiles. In a small bowl, beat egg whites until stiff; fold into mixture. Pour into 6 lightly buttered molds or custard dishes; set in a pan of hot water. Bake at 325° for 30 minutes or until set. Remove from oven and turn out onto serving plates.

Serves 6.

Acorn Squash Stuffed
with Cranberries

2 ACORN SQUASH
1/2 cup fresh CRANBERRIES
1/2 cup chopped NUTS
1/2 tsp. CINNAMON

2 Tbsp. MARGARINE, melted
1/2 cup packed BROWN
    SUGAR

Cut squash in half lengthwise and remove seeds. In a bowl, combine remaining ingredients. Fill squash halves with cranberry mixture. Bake at 350° for 50 minutes or until squash is tender.

Serves 4.

Spaghetti Squash with Mushrooms

1 SPAGHETTI SQUASH
1/4 cup PARSLEY, chopped
1/4 cup OLIVE OIL
5 Tbsp. BUTTER or MARGARINE
2 cloves GARLIC, minced
1/2 lb. fresh MUSHROOMS, sliced
1/4 cup grated PARMESAN CHEESE
SALT and PEPPER to taste

Pierce squash in several places to allow evaporation while cooking. Place whole squash in microwave oven and cook on High for 15 minutes, turning once or twice. Remove from microwave and let stand for 10 minutes. In a small bowl, place parsley, olive oil, 2 tablespoons of the butter and garlic. Cook on High for 1 minute; remove and set aside. In a skillet, sauté mushrooms in remaining 3 tablespoons butter. Cut squash in half lengthwise and remove seeds. With a fork, gently pull flesh from squash and place in a large bowl. Add mushrooms and pour butter mixture over top. Sprinkle with cheese, salt and pepper. Stir and serve.

Spaghetti Squash or Vegetable Spaghetti?

Familiar to many by either name, this creamy-colored watermelon-shaped winter squash earned its name because, when cooked, the flesh separates into spaghetti-like strands. When choosing this squash, avoid those that have a greenish color (indicates not mature). Spaghetti squash can be stored, at room temperature, for 2-3 weeks. Serve as a side dish, in a casserole or add to your favorite salad.

Zucchini in Creamy Dill Sauce

1/2 tsp. CHICKEN BOUILLON GRANULES
1/3 cup LIGHT SOUR CREAM
2 Tbsp. OLIVE OIL
1/3 cup coarsely chopped ONION
1 clove GARLIC, minced
2-3 sm. ZUCCHINI, quartered lengthwise and
    cut into 2-inch pieces
1 tsp. dried DILL

In a small bowl, combine bouillon and sour cream; set aside. In a large skillet, preheat oil for 2 minutes. Add onions and sauté for 2 minutes, stirring frequently. Add garlic and zucchini pieces. Stir and cook just until zucchini is crisp-tender. Spoon sour cream mixture over zucchini; sprinkle with dill weed. Toss to coat thoroughly and cook just until heated through (cream will separate if boiled). Serve at once.

Serves 4-6.

Cranberry Acorn Squash

4 sm. ACORN SQUASH

Cranberry Compote:
   1 1/2 cups whole CRANBERRIES   1/2 cup packed MAPLE
   1/2 cup APPLESAUCE   or BROWN SUGAR
   1/2 tsp. grated ORANGE PEEL   1/2 cup RAISINS
   3 tsp. COOKING OIL   1/2 cup WALNUTS

Preheat oven to 350°. Cut each squash in half lengthwise and remove seeds. Place squash, cut-side-down, in an oiled baking dish. Bake for 35 minutes or until tender; set aside to cool. In a bowl, combine all compote ingredients and mix well. Spoon compote into squash; return to oven and bake for an additional 25-30 minutes.

Serves 8.

Vegetable Pie

2 Tbsp. VEGETABLE OIL
2 cloves GARLIC, chopped
3 med. TOMATOES, chopped
2 sm. ONIONS, chopped
1 sm. EGGPLANT, peeled,
  quartered and sliced
1 sm. GREEN BELL
  PEPPER, sliced

1 cup CORN
SALT and PEPPER to taste
3 ZUCCHINI, sliced
6 Tbsp. grated PARMESAN
  CHEESE
1 (9-inch) unbaked PIE SHELL
2 Tbsp. BUTTER, cut into
  pieces

Preheat oven to 350°. In a large skillet, heat oil; add garlic, tomatoes, onion, eggplant, bell pepper, corn, salt and pepper. Sauté until vegetables are crisp-tender. Stir in zucchini and continue to cook until zucchini is crisp-tender. Sprinkle 2 tablespoons of the Parmesan cheese over bottom of pie shell. Using a slotted spoon, add 1/2 of the vegetables to pie shell. Sprinkle with another 2 tablespoons of the Parmesan cheese and dot with 1 tablespoon of the butter. Add remaining vegetables; sprinkle with remaining Parmesan cheese and dot with remaining butter. Bake for 40 minutes or until crust is golden brown. Serve hot.

Serves 6-8.

Veggie Kabobs

CHERRY TOMATOES
ONIONS, cut into 1-inch chunks
GREEN, RED AND YELLOW BELL PEPPERS,
  cut into 1/2-inch wide strips
1 can (20 oz.) PINEAPPLE CHUNKS
ZUCCHINI, cut into 1/4-inch slices
MUSHROOMS
CAULIFLOWER, cut into chunks

Carefully skewer vegetables, wrapping pepper strips around pineapple to secure. Season to taste and marinate, if desired. Grill over medium heat until cooked and slightly crisp.

Zucchini Puff

2 1/2 Tbsp. BUTTER
1 med. ONION, thinly sliced
2 ZUCCHINI, cut into
   1/2-inch slices
4 lg. EGGS

2 Tbsp. WATER
SALT and PEPPER
1/2 cup shredded CHEDDAR
   or SWISS CHEESE

Preheat broiler to 400°. In a large heavy skillet, melt 2 tablespoons of the butter; add onion and sauté until onions are translucent. Add zucchini and continue to cook, stirring occasionally, until onions and zucchini are slightly browned. In a bowl, beat eggs with water; add salt and pepper to taste and stir into zucchini mixture. Cook over medium heat until partially done. Run extra butter around rim of skillet and sprinkle cheddar cheese on top. Place skillet under broiler. Watch carefully—the soufflé will puff up, the cheese will melt and the top will turn golden. Serve immediately.

Serves 4.

Rice Casserole

1 tsp. VEGETABLE OIL
1 (8 oz.) TOFU CAKE, mashed
1 ONION, diced
2 CARROTS, diced
1 RED BELL PEPPER, diced
2 ZUCCHINI, chopped
8 oz. fresh MUSHROOMS, sliced
4 cups cooked BROWN RICE
1 BEET, diced

1 Tbsp. GARLIC POWDER
1 Tbsp. MARGARINE
1 Tbsp. TAMARI
1 cup WATER
8 oz. MONTEREY JACK
   CHEESE, grated
Dash of BLACK PEPPER
1 tsp. PAPRIKA

In a large skillet, heat oil and sauté tofu, onion, carrots and bell pepper for 10 minutes. Add zucchini and mushrooms and cook for 8 minutes. In a large bowl, combine all ingredients and mix well. Pour into an oiled casserole dish and cover with foil. Bake at 350° for 45 minutes.

Serves 6.

Baked Acorn Squash with Pineapple Glaze

1 ACORN SQUASH	1 Tbsp. slivered ALMONDS
2 tsp. BUTTER	1 Tbsp. chopped MARASCHINO
SALT and PEPPER	CHERRIES
4 Tbsp. CRUSHED	2 tsp. CHERRY JUICE
PINEAPPLE drained	2 tsp. ORANGE JUICE
2 tsp. BROWN SUGAR	

Wash acorn squash and cut in half lengthwise; scrape out seeds and coarse pulp. Rub the inside of each half with butter; sprinkle with salt and pepper to taste. Place cut-side-down on a well-greased baking pan. Bake at 400° for 30 minutes. In a bowl, combine pineapple, brown sugar, almonds, cherries and juices. Turn squash over and fill each half with pineapple mixture. Cover with foil and continue baking for 30 minutes or until squash centers are soft. Remove squash from oven and pour *Pineapple Glaze* evenly over top of each.

Pineapple Glaze

1 cup PINEAPPLE JUICE	1 1/2 Tbsp. CORNSTARCH
1 tsp. grated ORANGE RIND	1 Tbsp. BROWN SUGAR
1 tsp. grated LIME RIND	

Blend glaze ingredients in a saucepan. Cook over medium heat and stir until thickened. Let stand for 5-7 minutes.

Serves 4.

How to Make Acorn Squash Candles!

Cut off the top of the squash and scrape out pulp and flesh. In the center of the squash, using one-fourth of a toothpick, embed a wick that is long enough to extend above the top. Lay a pencil or other support across the top of the squash and tape or secure the wick to it. Pour tinted melted paraffin inside of shell. When paraffin has hardened, peel away the shell.

Apple Butternut Bake

1 lg. BUTTERNUT SQUASH
1/4 cup + 2 Tbsp. BUTTER
1 Tbsp. BROWN SUGAR
1/4 tsp. SALT

Dash of PEPPER
1/2 cup SUGAR
1 1/2 qts. TART APPLES,
    peeled, cored and sliced

Topping:
   3 cups coarsely crushed CORN FLAKES
   1/2 cup chopped PECANS
   2 Tbsp. BUTTER, melted
   1 cup packed BROWN SUGAR

Bake squash at 350° for 30 minutes or until tender. Cut in half; remove and discard seeds. Scrape flesh into a large bowl and mash until smooth. Stir in 1/4 cup butter, brown sugar, salt and pepper; set aside. In a large skillet, melt 2 tablespoons butter and add sugar and apples. Simmer over low heat until apples are just tender. Spread apples in a large flat baking dish. Spoon squash over apples. Mix together ingredients for topping and spread over squash. Bake at 350° for 30 minutes or until heated through and topping is light brown.

Serves 4.

Grilled Zucchini

2 lbs. ZUCCHINI, peeled
   and sliced
2 TOMATOES, diced
1 ONION, thinly sliced
1 1/2 tsp. SALT

1/2 tsp. PEPPER
1/2 tsp. dried BASIL
1/2 tsp. OREGANO
3 Tbsp. BUTTER

Place zucchini, tomatoes and onion in the center of a large square of heavy-duty aluminum foil (or 2 layers of regular foil). Sprinkle with spices and dot with butter. Wrap foil around vegetables and seal tightly. Grill over medium heat for 30-40 minutes, shaking occasionally.

Serves 4-6.

Apple-Stuffed Acorn Squash

2 ACORN SQUASH

Stuffing:

2 Tbsp. UNSALTED BUTTER
1/2 cup finely chopped ONIONS
1 cup peeled and chopped
   APPLES

2 Tbsp. BROWN SUGAR
1 Tbsp. BALSAMIC VINEGAR
1/2 tsp. dried THYME
1/4 tsp. SALT

Split acorn squash in half lengthwise and remove seeds and pulp. Place squash in a baking dish; set aside. To prepare stuffing: Melt butter in a skillet and sauté onions for 3-4 minutes over medium heat. Add apples, brown sugar, vinegar, thyme and salt; continue to sauté for 2-3 minutes. Remove from heat. Pierce or score squash before filling so more of the flavor of the stuffing is absorbed. Spoon stuffing mixture into the squash. Bake at 375° for 1 hour or until squash is tender.

Note: To keep squash moist while baking, add 1/2 inch of water to the bottom of baking pan; place squash in pan and cover with foil.

Serves 4-6.

Coconut-Curry Zucchini

3 Tbsp. BUTTER
2 cups cubed ZUCCHINI
1/2 cup minced ONION
1 clove GARLIC, crushed
1/3 cup RAISINS
2 Tbsp. FLOUR

1 cup WATER
1 cube CHICKEN BOUILLON,
   crushed
1 tsp. CURRY, or to taste
SALT
1/4 cup shredded COCONUT

In a large skillet, melt 1 tablespoon of the butter and sauté zucchini, onion and garlic until almost tender; remove to a warm dish. Stir raisins into zucchini mixture. Melt remaining butter in skillet; whisk in flour. When golden, slowly stir in water and bouillon and continue to stir until sauce thickens. Add curry, salt to taste and zucchini and simmer for 1 minute. Place in a serving dish and garnish with coconut.

Serves 6.

Baked Acorn Squash

3 lg. ACORN SQUASH
1 cup WATER
1 can (13.5 oz) PINEAPPLE
    TIDBITS
1 1/2 cups diced, unpeeled
    RED APPLES
1 cup chopped CELERY

1/2 cup chopped WALNUTS
1/4 cup BUTTER
1/2 cup packed BROWN
    SUGAR
1/2 tsp. CINNAMON
1/4 tsp. SALT

Cut squash in half lengthwise and scoop out seeds. Place cut-side-down in a large glass baking dish. Add water to the bottom of dish. Bake at 350° for 45 minutes. In a small bowl, combine pineapple, apples, celery and walnuts. In a saucepan, melt butter and blend in brown sugar, cinnamon and salt. Pour brown sugar mixture over pineapple mixture and stir gently. Remove squash from oven; drain off water and turn cut-side-up. Spoon pineapple mixture into squash and return to oven. Bake for an additional 15-20 minutes or until squash is tender.

Serves 6.

Herbed Squash Casserole

6 cups sliced ZUCCHINI or YELLOW SQUASH
1/4 cup chopped ONION
1 can (10.75 oz.) CREAM OF CHICKEN SOUP
1 cup SOUR CREAM
1 cup shredded CARROTS
1/2 cup BUTTER, melted
1 pkg. (6 oz.) HERB STUFFING MIX

In a saucepan, bring 6 cups of water to a boil. Add squash and onion and boil for 5 minutes; drain. In a large bowl, combine soup, sour cream and carrots. Stir in squash mixture. In a separate bowl, add butter to stuffing mix and toss. Layer 1/2 of the stuffing in a 12 x 8 baking dish. Pour squash mixture over top and sprinkle with remaining stuffing. Bake at 350° for 30 minutes.

Serves 8.

Lemon Zucchini

3-4 lbs. ZUCCHINI, sliced
1 Tbsp. SALT
1/4 cup BUTTER
2 Tbsp. INSTANT MINCED ONIONS
1/2 tsp. grated LEMON PEEL
3 Tbsp. fresh LEMON JUICE

In a large saucepan, cover zucchini with water. Add salt, cover and bring to a boil. Continue boiling until zucchini is crisp-tender; drain and place in a large bowl. In a saucepan, melt butter; add minced onion, lemon peel and juice and stir. Pour mixture over zucchini; mix and serve.

Serves 6-8.

Corn-Stuffed Squash

4 ACORN SQUASH
1 Tbsp. VEGETABLE OIL
1 med. ONION, finely chopped
3/4 cup RICOTTA CHEESE
1 cup CORN
1/2 cup grated PARMESAN CHEESE
SALT and PEPPER

In a saucepan, cover squash with water and boil until tender; remove and rinse with ice water. Cut off stems and scoop out seeds and flesh, keeping shell intact. Chop flesh and set aside. In a large skillet, heat oil and sauté onion until translucent. Add squash and cook until liquid has evaporated. Remove from heat and cool. In a bowl, blend squash with ricotta cheese, corn, and 1/4 cup of the Parmesan cheese. Season with salt and pepper to taste. Generously fill shells with squash mixture; place in baking dish and top with remaining Parmesan cheese. Bake at 350° for 40-45 minutes.

Serves 4-6.

Savory Skillet Squash

4 slices BACON
1/4 cup chopped ONION
1/4 cup chopped CELERY
1/4 cup chopped GREEN
   BELL PEPPER
1/2 cup uncooked INSTANT RICE
2 cups chopped ZUCCHINI

2 cups chopped TOMATOES
1/8 tsp. OREGANO
1/4 tsp. PEPPER
1 1/2 tsp. SALT
1/8 tsp. THYME
1 cup shredded CHEDDAR
   CHEESE

In a large skillet, cook bacon until crisp; remove and set aside. Heat bacon drippings and sauté onion, celery and bell pepper until tender. Add rice and stir well to coat. Stir in zucchini, tomatoes and seasonings. Cook, covered, until rice is tender. Remove cover, sprinkle with cheddar cheese, replace cover and cook until cheese melts. Crumble bacon over casserole before serving.

Serves 4-6.

Sweet Tater Challenge

Many people like sweet potatoes, but dislike winter squash. With this dish, you won't be able to tell the difference!

6 slices BACON, diced
3 Tbsp. BUTTER
1/4 cup PECANS
1 clove GARLIC, minced
1 BUTTERNUT SQUASH, peeled
   and diced into 1-inch cubes

1/2 cup dried CRANBERRIES
1 SWEET ONION, large diced
1/4 cup WATER
1/4 cup packed LIGHT BROWN
   SUGAR

In a nonstick skillet, fry bacon until crisp; set aside. Drain most of the drippings from skillet; add 1 tablespoon butter and pecans. Cook and stir over medium heat until pecans are lightly toasted; set aside. Add garlic, squash, cranberries, onion and water to skillet. Steam gently until squash is almost tender. Add brown sugar and remaining butter. When syrup has thickened, coat all ingredients generously. Place mixture in a serving dish and sprinkle top with bacon and pecans.

Squash Dressing Casserole

2 Tbsp. BUTTER
1 cup diced ONION
1 cup diced CELERY
1 cup diced GREEN BELL PEPPER
1 pkg. (15 oz.) JIFFY® CORNBREAD MIX, baked
2 cups MILK
2 lbs. YELLOW SQUASH, cooked, mashed and seasoned
1 can (10.75 oz.) CREAM OF CHICKEN SOUP
1 tsp. SAGE
SALT and PEPPER to taste
1 cup shredded CHEDDAR CHEESE

In a saucepan, melt butter and sauté onion, celery and bell pepper until onion is translucent. In a large bowl, crumble cornbread into milk and mix lightly. Combine squash, cornbread mixture, sautéed vegetables, soup, sage, salt and pepper. Pour into a greased casserole dish; sprinkle with cheddar cheese. Bake at 350° for 1 hour.

Serves 10.

Cheesy Zucchini

4 cups diced ZUCCHINI
3 EGGS, lightly beaten
1 cup MILK
1/4 cup BUTTER or MARGARINE, melted
1 jar (4 oz.) PIMENTOS, drained and chopped
1 1/2 cups crushed CHEESE CRACKERS or SALTINES
2 cups shredded SHARP CHEDDAR CHEESE
PAPRIKA

In a saucepan, cook zucchini in boiling salted water for 5 minutes; drain. In a bowl, combine remaining ingredients except for the paprika. Add zucchini and mix well. Pour into an 11 x 7 baking dish; sprinkle with paprika. Bake at 300° for 25-30 minutes until browned and bubbling.

Serves 8.

Baked Butternut Squash and Parsnips

2 BUTTERNUT SQUASH
1 1/2 lbs. PARSNIPS
2 Tbsp. BUTTER
2 med. ONIONS, thinly sliced
1 Tbsp. OLIVE OIL
2 sm. ORANGES, peeled, seeded
   and coarsely chopped

2 Tbsp. HONEY
2/3 cup WHITE WINE
1/3 cup CHICKEN STOCK
1/2 tsp. NUTMEG
SALT and PEPPER
3/4 cup grated PARMESAN
   CHEESE

Cut squash in half, remove seeds, peel and cut into 1/2-inch cubes; place in a saucepan with enough salted water to cover. Boil until just tender. Peel parsnips and cut into 1/4-inch rounds. Add parsnips to saucepan and boil for 1 minute. Drain, place in a bowl and set aside. In a skillet, melt butter and sauté onions until lightly browned; combine with squash and parsnips. In a blender, purée the oranges, honey, wine, stock and nutmeg. Add to vegetable mixture, season with salt and pepper to taste and toss gently to combine. Sprinkle cheese evenly over top of mixture when ready to serve.

Serves 6.

Savory Yellow Squash

3 strips BACON, diced
1 ONION, diced
2 lbs. YELLOW SQUASH,
   cut into rounds

1/4 cup WATER
2 Tbsp. BUTTER
SALT and PEPPER to taste

In a skillet over medium heat, cook bacon until lightly browned. Add onion and sauté until onion is translucent. Add squash and cook for two minutes; stir. Add water and cover. Reduce heat to low and simmer for 10 minutes or until squash is tender. Add butter, salt and pepper.

Serves 6.

Zucchini Parmigiana

1 Tbsp. BUTTER
2 Tbsp. OIL
1 lg. ZUCCHINI, sliced into 1/2-inch thick rounds
1 med. EGGPLANT, peeled and sliced
1 lg. ONION, coarsely chopped
1 tsp. SALT
1/2 tsp. PEPPER
1 tsp. OREGANO
1 can (15 oz.) TOMATO SAUCE
1 clove GARLIC, crushed
8 oz. MOZZARELLA CHEESE, sliced
2 Tbsp. grated PARMESAN CHEESE

Preheat oven to 375°. In a large skillet, melt butter and stir in oil. Add vegetables and cook for 10 minutes or until just tender, stirring occasionally. Stir in salt, pepper and oregano. Spoon mixture into a greased 2-quart baking dish. In a bowl, mix tomato sauce with garlic and pour over vegetables. Tuck mozzarella cheese slices into vegetables so that half of each slice is on the surface; sprinkle with Parmesan cheese. Bake casserole for 25 minutes or until cheese is hot and bubbly.

Serves 4.

Pattypan Olé

1 lb. PATTYPAN SQUASH, cut into 1/4-inch pieces
1/2 cup MAYONNAISE
1 can (4 oz.) diced GREEN CHILES
1/2 cup grated CHEDDAR CHEESE
1/2 cup BREAD CRUMBS
Dash of TABASCO®

In a saucepan, cover squash with water and cook until just tender; drain well. Stir in remaining ingredients and mix gently. Serve hot.

Serves 4.

Zucchini Casserole

4 Tbsp. BUTTER, reserve 2 Tbsp.
4 ZUCCHINI, thinly sliced
2 med. ONIONS, thinly sliced
3 lg. fresh TOMATOES
2 Tbsp. SUGAR
1 Tbsp. TURMERIC
SALT and freshly ground BLACK PEPPER
1/3 cup grated PARMESAN CHEESE

Preheat oven to 300°. In a large skillet, melt 2 tablespoons butter and sauté zucchini, for 15 minutes. Add remaining butter and onion to skillet and sauté zucchini until tender. Briefly immerse tomatoes in boiling water (about 30 seconds); let cool slightly. Peel and dice tomatoes and place in a bowl. Mix with sugar, turmeric, salt and pepper. Pour zucchini mixture into a large casserole dish.* Pour tomato mixture over top of zucchini; sprinkle with Parmesan cheese. Cover and bake for 25 minutes or until cheese melts and the mixture bubbles. Serve hot.

Serves 4-6.

*For a full-meal variation of this recipe, add a pound of cooked ground beef to the bottom of a casserole dish and continue with directions above.

Sour Cream & Dill Zucchini

1/2 cup BUTTER
3 cups thinly sliced ZUCCHINI
2 Tbsp. chopped fresh DILL

SALT and PEPPER to taste
1 cup SOUR CREAM

In a saucepan, melt butter and sauté zucchini for 1 minute. Sprinkle with dill, salt and pepper. Cook until zucchini is tender. Gently stir in sour cream. Heat through.

Serves 6-8.

Zucchini-Potato Bake

2 Tbsp. VEGETABLE OIL
1 GREEN BELL PEPPER, diced
2 ONIONS, sliced
2 cloves GARLIC, minced
1 ZUCCHINI, thinly sliced
2 cups TOMATO SAUCE
1 Tbsp. TAMARI

1 tsp. BASIL
Dash of CAYENNE
1 pkg. (16 oz.) frozen HASH
    BROWNS, thawed
1/2 cup grated MONTEREY
    JACK CHEESE
2 Tbsp. BREAD CRUMBS

In a large skillet, heat oil and sauté bell pepper, onion, garlic and zucchini until tender. Add 1 1/2 cups tomato sauce, tamari, basil and cayenne to sautéed vegetables and stir. Spread remaining tomato sauce in bottom of a casserole dish. Add a layer of 1/2 of the potatoes. Sprinkle top with 1/4 cup of cheese and 1/2 of the sauté mixture. Repeat layers with remaining potatoes and sauté mixture. Top with the remaining cheese; sprinkle with bread crumbs and bake at 350° for 30 minutes.

Serves 4.

Creamed Squash

4 cups sliced YELLOW SQUASH
1/2 cup chopped ONION
1/2 cup WATER
8 oz. SOUR CREAM
1/2 tsp. SALT
1/4 tsp. PEPPER
1/4 tsp. dried BASIL

1 cup SOFT BREAD CRUMBS
1/2 cup shredded CHEDDAR
    CHEESE
1/4 cup BUTTER, melted
1/2 tsp. PAPRIKA
8 slices BACON, cooked and
    crumbled

In a saucepan, cook squash and onion in boiling water until tender; drain. In a bowl, mash squash and combine with sour cream, salt, pepper and basil. Pour mixture into a greased 2-quart casserole dish. In a bowl, combine bread crumbs, cheddar cheese, butter and paprika; sprinkle over squash mixture. Top with bacon. Bake at 300° for 20 minutes.

Serves 6.

Squash Casserole

8 YELLOW SQUASH, sliced
1 Tbsp. BUTTER
1 med. ONION, finely chopped
1 GREEN BELL PEPPER, chopped
1 RED BELL PEPPER, chopped
1 1/2 cups grated MOZZARELLA CHEESE
1 cup grated CHEDDAR CHEESE
1 cup BREAD CRUMBS

Boil or steam squash until tender; drain. In a large skillet, melt butter and sauté onion and bell peppers until tender. Spread squash in a 13 x 9 casserole dish. In a bowl, combine mozzarella cheese and cheddar cheese. Cover squash with 3/4 of the cheese mixture and 3/4 cup of the sautéed mixture. Cover with bread crumbs and sprinkle with remaining cheese and bell pepper mixture. Bake at 350° for 30 minutes.

Serves 4-6.

Zucchini is Clearly Good for You!

Zucchini contains lutein and xeazanthin, which are carotenoids that help protect against cataracts and macular degeneration, which can cause blindness.

Corn & Zucchini Casserole

3/4 cup grated ZUCCHINI
1 can (15.25 oz.) CORN
1 cup chopped GREEN ONION
3/4 cup grated CARROT
1/2 cup grated CHEDDAR CHEESE

1/2 cup OATS
2 Tbsp. BUTTER, melted
4 EGGS, beaten
SALT and PEPPER to taste

Preheat oven to 300°. In a large bowl, combine all ingredients and mix well. Pour into a greased 8 x 8 baking pan. Bake for 35-40 minutes.

Serves 4.

Ratatouille

2 Tbsp. OLIVE OIL
1 ONION, coarsely chopped
1-2 cloves GARLIC, minced
1 EGGPLANT, diced
2 ZUCCHINI, sliced
1 BELL PEPPER, diced

1 can (14.5 oz.) S&W® ITALIAN
   REDI CUT TOMATOES
1/4 tsp. BASIL
1/4 tsp. OREGANO
SALT and PEPPER to taste
PARMESAN CHEESE

In a large skillet, heat oil and sauté onion, garlic and eggplant for 10 minutes. Add zucchini and bell pepper; sauté an additional 10 minutes. Stir in tomatoes and seasonings. Gently simmer until vegetables are tender. When ready to serve, sprinkle with Parmesan cheese.

Serves 4.

Squash in Orange Cream Sauce

1 lb. YELLOW SQUASH, thinly sliced
1 lb. ZUCCHINI, thinly sliced
2 Tbsp. BUTTER
2 Tbsp. frozen ORANGE JUICE CONCENTRATE, thawed
1 cup SOUR CREAM
2 Tbsp. FLOUR
Sprigs of PARSLEY

In a saucepan, bring a small amount of salted water to a boil and add yellow squash and zucchini. Cover and cook for 8-10 minutes; drain. In a saucepan, melt butter and stir in orange concentrate. Heat until just warm. In a bowl, combine sour cream and flour and then stir into orange sauce. Heat, but do not boil. When serving, pour sauce over squash. Garnish with parsley.

Serves 4.

Golden Squash Casserole

1 lb. fresh or frozen CORN KERNELS
1 lb. fresh or frozen GREEN BEANS
4 cups diced YELLOW SQUASH
1 pint (16 oz.) SOUR CREAM
2 EGGS
4 Tbsp. MARGARINE, melted
1 cup CORNMEAL
1/2 cup sliced JALAPEÑO PEPPERS
1/2 cup shredded MONTEREY JACK CHEESE

In a large bowl, combine corn and green beans and toss lightly. Stir in squash. In a large mixing bowl, mix sour cream and eggs together. Add vegetables and remaining ingredients and mix well. Pour into a greased baking dish. Bake at 350° for 45 minutes or until golden brown.

Serves 4-6.

Did You Know?

In Mexico many types of squash and pumpkins are called "calabaza" and zucchini are often referred to as "calabacitas." As you can see, there are quite a few recipe variations with the same name.

Carrot-Zucchini Frittata

3 Tbsp. BUTTER
1 clove GARLIC, minced
2 ZUCCHINI, grated
2 lg. CARROTS, grated
4 EGGS, beaten

SALT and PEPPER, to taste
1/3 cup grated PARMESAN
    CHEESE
CAYENNE to taste

In an oven-proof skillet, melt butter and sauté garlic. Stir in zucchini and carrots and cook until tender. Stir in eggs and remaining ingredients. Bake in a 350° oven for 15 minutes or until set. Sprinkle with additional Parmesan cheese.

Serves 6-8.

Summertime Casserole

2 Tbsp. MARGARINE
2 Tbsp. finely chopped ONION
1/4 cup SOUR CREAM
1/2 cup grated SHARP CHEDDAR CHEESE
3 EGGS
1/2 tsp. SALT
Dash of PEPPER
Dash of NUTMEG
1 1/2 cups HALF and HALF
3 SUMMER SQUASH, sliced, cooked, well-drained
1/2 cup CRACKER CRUMBS

In a large skillet, melt margarine and sauté onion until golden. Remove skillet from heat and stir in sour cream. Add cheddar cheese; return to low heat and stir until cheese melts. In a bowl, beat eggs, spices and half and half together. Add to onion mixture. Place squash in a greased 2 1/2-quart casserole dish. Pour onion mixture over top and sprinkle with cracker crumbs. Bake at 350° for 30 minutes.

Serves 4.

Did You Know?

Native Americans traditionally grew squash, beans and corn together. Corn stalks provided support for the bean plants and squash vines provided ground cover which kept the soil moist. These three foods were known as the "sustainers of life" and were referred to spiritually as the "Three Sisters."

Creamy Zucchini Bake

4 ZUCCHINI
4 oz. CREAM CHEESE
1/3 cup SOUR CREAM
SALT and PEPPER to taste
1/4 cup thinly sliced GREEN ONIONS
Dash of CRUSHED RED PEPPER
PAPRIKA to garnish

In a saucepan, parboil zucchini whole for 5-7 minutes; cool in cold running water. Cut zucchini in half lengthwise and scoop pulp into a bowl. Add remaining ingredients (except paprika) to pulp and mix well. Spoon mixture back into zucchini shells; sprinkle with paprika. Bake at 350° for 30 minutes or until lightly browned.

Serves 2-4.

Crunchy Zucchini-Tomato Bake

3 cups sliced ZUCCHINI
1 can (16 oz.) STEWED TOMATOES
1 1/2 cups SEASONED SALAD CROUTONS
1 can (2.5 oz) FRENCH-FRIED ONION RINGS
1/2 cup shredded CHEDDAR CHEESE

Spread zucchini in a shallow baking pan and layer tomatoes over the top. Sprinkle croutons and onion rings evenly over the tomatoes. Bake at 350° for 25 minutes. Sprinkle cheese over the top of the casserole and bake for an additional 10 minutes or until cheese is melted and lightly browned.

Serves 4.

Calabacitas

2-3 Tbsp. BUTTER
1/2 lg. SWEET SPANISH or WHITE ONION, thinly sliced
2 cups (appx. 4 ears) fresh CORN, cut from the cobs
2 cups thinly sliced ZUCCHINI
2 oz. MOZZARELLA CHEESE, thinly sliced

In a skillet, melt butter and sauté onion, corn and zucchini over low heat until zucchini is tender. Layer cheese on top of mixture; cover and continue cooking until cheese melts. Serve immediately.

Serves 4.

Chayote, Mirliton or Vegetable Pear?

An increasingly popular summer squash is the chayote (chy-o-tay). Also called mirliton, vegetable pear and christophene it has a large, soft central seed and a fairly thick, deeply ridged skin. When using in place of other summer squash, increase cooking time by five minutes.

Calabacitas II

6 ZUCCHINI, peeled and sliced
1 med. ONION, chopped
2 cloves GARLIC, minced
1 lg. TOMATO, diced
1 can (15.25 oz.) CORN
1 can (16 oz.) STEWED TOMATOES
SALT and PEPPER to taste
3/4 cup shredded MONTEREY JACK CHEESE

Preheat oven to 350°. In a bowl, combine all ingredients, except cheese and pour into a casserole dish. Cover and bake for 20 minutes or until vegetables are tender. Remove from heat and sprinkle with cheese.

Serves 6-8.

Calabacitas con Crema

(Squash with Cream)

Every New Mexican family has their own version of this popular dish. What every recipe has in common is squash cooked with chiles. This version is enriched with cream and traditional herbs. Fresh corn kernels are common additions to this dish.

3/4 lb. ZUCCHINI, diced
1 TOMATO, chopped
SALT and PEPPER
2 Tbsp. minced fresh CILANTRO LEAVES
2 cloves GARLIC, minced
1 Tbsp. minced fresh MINT LEAVES
3/4 tsp. CINNAMON
1/3 cup roasted, peeled and chopped NEW MEXICO GREEN
    CHILES
1/4 cup LIGHT CREAM

In a large heavy saucepan, stir all the ingredients together. Cover and simmer over low heat for 30 minutes until the zucchini is tender and the sauce is creamy.

Serves 2-4.

Fried Squash Blossoms

12 lg. SQUASH BLOSSOMS
1/4 tsp. ground CUMIN
1/4 tsp. GARLIC SALT
1/2 cup FLOUR
1/2 tsp. BAKING POWDER

1 EGG
1/2 cup MILK
1 Tbsp. SALAD OIL
OIL for frying

Wash blossoms and then dry on paper towels; set aside. Sift dry ingredients together. In a bowl, beat together egg, milk and salad oil. Gradually mix egg mixture into dry ingredients. Heat oil in a deep fat fryer to 375°. Dip blossoms in batter and fry, a few at a time, until crisp. Drain on paper towels.

Serves 4.

Zucchini Supreme

1 Tbsp. SOY SAUCE
6 EGG WHITES
3 cups shredded ZUCCHINI
3/4 cup WHOLE-WHEAT FLOUR
1/4 cup toasted WHEAT GERM
1/2 cup shredded PARMESAN
   CHEESE
1/2 cup finely chopped ONION

2 Tbsp. chopped fresh
   PARSLEY
1/2 tsp. ITALIAN SEASONING
2 cloves GARLIC, minced
1 tsp. BUTTER-FLAVORED
   SALT
1/2 tsp. PEPPER
1 tsp. BAKING SODA

Preheat oven to 350°. Prepare 13 x 9 casserole dish with cooking spray. In a bowl, beat soy sauce and egg whites until peaks form. In a separate bowl, combine remaining ingredients and blend well. Fold into egg white mixture. Gently pour into casserole dish. Bake for 25-30 minutes or until top is lightly browned. Cut into squares and serve warm.

Serves 8.

Winter Squash Relish

2 cups WATER
1 tsp. SALT
2/3 cup peeled and diced ACORN SQUASH
1/3 cup diced CELERY
1/3 cup diced RED BELL PEPPER
1 tsp. finely grated ORANGE PEEL
1 tsp. chopped fresh SAGE
1 tsp. chopped fresh THYME
2 tsp. LEMON JUICE
SALT
CAYENNE

In a small saucepan, add salt to water and bring to a boil. Add squash and cook for 2 minutes or until tender. Strain squash and place under cool running water for 20 seconds to stop the cooking process. In a bowl, combine squash, celery, bell pepper, orange peel, herbs and lemon juice. Season with salt and cayenne to taste.

Zucchini Relish

4 cups chopped ONION
3 1/2 cups chopped GREEN
   BELL PEPPER
2 1/2 cups grated ZUCCHINI
5 Tbsp. SALT
2 1/2 cups VINEGAR
3/4 tsp. CORNSTARCH

6 cups SUGAR
3/4 tsp. TURMERIC
1 Tbsp. DRY MUSTARD
1/2 tsp. CELERY SEEDS
3/4 tsp. NUTMEG
1/2 tsp. PEPPER

In a large mixing bowl, combine onion, bell pepper, zucchini and salt; let stand overnight and then drain. In a large saucepan, heat remaining ingredients to boiling. Add vegetable mixture and cook slowly until vegetables are tender. While hot, pour into sterilized jars and seal according to manufacturer's directions.

Zucchini Tomato Sauce

2 Tbsp. BUTTER
3 ZUCCHINI, sliced
2 cups chopped TOMATOES

SALT and PEPPER
1 cup grated MOZZARELLA
   CHEESE

In a skillet, melt butter and sauté zucchini until tender. Add tomatoes and season with salt and pepper to taste. Cook for 10 minutes until tomatoes are tender. Stir in cheese and continue cooking until cheese has melted.

Fresh Squash Salsa

4 TOMATOES, diced
1 ZUCCHINI, diced
1 YELLOW SQUASH, diced
1 jar (4 oz.) PIMENTOS,
   drained and diced

2 sm. JALAPEÑO or SERRANO
   CHILES, diced
2 Tbsp. OLIVE OIL
2 Tbsp. LIME JUICE
1/3 cup chopped fresh CILANTRO

In a large bowl, combine all the ingredients and mix well. Cover and refrigerate overnight.

Makes 2 cups.

Breads
&
Desserts

Choco-Nut Zucchini Bread

3 EGGS
2 cups SUGAR
1 cup SALAD OIL
2 oz. UNSWEETENED
    CHOCOLATE
1 tsp. VANILLA
2 cups grated ZUCCHINI

3 cups FLOUR
1 tsp. SALT
1 tsp. CINNAMON
1/4 tsp. BAKING POWDER
1 tsp. BAKING SODA
1 cup chopped ALMONDS

In a mixing bowl, beat eggs and stir in sugar and oil. In a double boiler, melt chocolate over hot water. Stir chocolate, vanilla and zucchini into egg mixture. In a separate bowl, combine flour with salt, cinnamon, baking powder and baking soda. Add dry ingredients to zucchini mixture. Add almonds and mix well. Pour into 2 well-oiled 9 x 5 loaf pans. Bake at 350° for 1 hour and 20 minutes or until loaves test done. Cool in pans for 15-20 minutes, then turn onto wire rack and cool thoroughly before slicing.

Zucchini Date Nut Bread

5 EGGS	1/2 tsp. BAKING SODA
2 cups packed BROWN SUGAR	3/4 tsp. BAKING POWDER
1 1/2 cups OIL	1 1/2 tsp. SALT
2 tsp. VANILLA	1 1/2 cups chopped WALNUTS
3 cups FLOUR	3 cups grated ZUCCHINI
1 1/2 Tbsp. CINNAMON	1 1/2 cups chopped DATES

In a mixing bowl, cream together eggs, brown sugar, oil and vanilla; set aside. In a separate bowl, combine flour, cinnamon, baking soda, baking powder and salt. Add dry ingredients to creamed mixture and mix until just moistened. Stir in zucchini and dates. Pour into 2 well-greased 9 x 5 loaf pans. Bake at 375° for 50-55 minutes or until loaves test done.

Did You Know?

April 25th is National Zucchini Bread Day!
Let's all celebrate and bake
some extra loaves!

Zucchini Cranberry Bread

3 EGGS	2 cups FLOUR
2 cups SUGAR	1 tsp. SALT
2 cups grated ZUCCHINI	2 tsp. BAKING SODA
1 cup OIL	2 tsp. CINNAMON
2 tsp. VANILLA	1 cup halved CRANBERRIES

In a mixing bowl, beat eggs. Stir in remaining ingredients and mix well. Pour into 2 (8 x 4) greased loaf pans or 4 "mini" loaf pans. Bake at 350° for 45-60 minutes. Bread is done when toothpick inserted in center comes out clean.

Zucchini & Fruit Bread

3 cups FLOUR
2 tsp. BAKING SODA
1/4 tsp. BAKING POWDER
1 tsp. SALT
1 1/2 tsp. CINNAMON
1/2 tsp. NUTMEG
3 EGGS
1 cup OIL

2 cups SUGAR
2 tsp. VANILLA
2 cups shredded ZUCCHINI
1 can (8 oz.) CRUSHED
    PINEAPPLE, drained
1 cup chopped NUTS
1 cup RAISINS, CURRANTS
    or DATES

In a bowl, combine flour, baking soda, baking powder, salt and spices. In a large bowl, beat eggs, oil, sugar and vanilla until thick. Stir in zucchini, pineapple and flour mixture and mix well. Add nuts and fruit. Pour into 2 greased 9 x 5 loaf pans. Bake at 325° for 1 hour. Bread is done when toothpick inserted into center comes out clean.

Zucchini Pecan Loaves

3 EGGS
1 3/4 cups SUGAR
1 cup SALAD OIL
2 3/4 tsp. VANILLA
2 cups grated ZUCCHINI
3 cups FLOUR

1 1/2 tsp. BAKING POWDER
2 tsp. BAKING SODA
1 tsp. SALT
3 tsp. CINNAMON
1 cup chopped PECANS

In a large bowl, beat eggs until fluffy. Add sugar, oil and vanilla and blend well. Stir in zucchini. In a separate bowl, combine flour, baking powder, baking soda, salt and cinnamon. Mix dry ingredients into creamed mixture. Stir in pecans. Pour into 3 greased 8 x 4 loaf pans. Bake at 350° for 1 hour.

Butternut Squash Loaf

2 cups FLOUR
1 Tbsp. BAKING POWDER
1 tsp. SALT
1/4 tsp. CINNAMON
1/4 tsp. GINGER
1/8 tsp. CLOVES
1/4 cup SUGAR
1/2 cup BROWN SUGAR

3/4 cup MILK
2 Tbsp. BUTTER
1 cup cooked, mashed
    BUTTERNUT SQUASH
1 EGG
1/2 cup chopped NUTS
1/3 cup RAISINS

In a mixing bowl, sift together flour, baking powder, salt, cinnamon, ginger, cloves, sugar and brown sugar. In a saucepan, heat milk and butter until butter is softened. Beat in butternut squash and egg. Add squash mixture to dry ingredients and mix until just moistened. Stir in nuts and raisins. Pour into a 9 x 5 greased loaf pan. Bake at 350° for 1 hour.

Zucchini Applesauce Bread

3 EGGS
1 cup unsweetened
    APPLESAUCE
2 cups SUGAR
2 tsp. VANILLA
2 cups shredded ZUCCHINI
1 cup CRUSHED PINEAPPLE,
    drained

3 cups ALL-PURPOSE FLOUR
2 tsp. BAKING SODA
1/2 tsp. BAKING POWDER
1 tsp. SALT
1 1/2 tsp. CINNAMON
3/4 cup RAISINS
1 cup chopped WALNUTS
    or PECANS

In a mixing bowl, beat together eggs, applesauce, sugar, and vanilla until fluffy. Stir in zucchini and pineapple. In a separate bowl, combine flour, baking soda, baking powder, salt and cinnamon. Add dry ingredients to applesauce mixture. Stir in raisins and nuts. Pour into 2 greased 9 x 5 loaf pans. Bake at 350° for 1 hour and 15 minutes.

Zucchini Raisin Bread

3 cups grated ZUCCHINI
2 1/2 cups SUGAR
1 cup OIL
1 cup chopped WALNUTS
1 1/2 tsp. CINNAMON
4 EGGS, slightly beaten

3 cups FLOUR
2 tsp. BAKING POWDER
1 tsp. BAKING SODA
1 tsp. SALT
1/2 cup RAISINS*

In a large bowl, combine all ingredients and mix well. Pour dough into a greased and floured 13 x 9 baking pan or 2 greased 9 x 5 loaf pans. Bake at 350° for 1 hour.

*May soak raisins in rum before adding.

Use it or Recycle it!

Instead of throwing away zucchini that have become too large in your garden, you can grate the large zucchini for use in zucchini breads or cut them up and put them in your compost bin to help make great soil for next year's crop!

Golden Squash Muffins

1 EGG
1 cup MILK
3/4 cup cooked YELLOW
   SQUASH
1/3 cup MARGARINE, room
   temperature
1/2 cup SUGAR

1 tsp. grated ORANGE PEEL
2 1/4 cups ALL-PURPOSE
   FLOUR
3 1/2 tsp. BAKING POWDER
1/2 tsp. SALT
1/4 cup GOLDEN RAISINS

Preheat oven to 375°. Place egg and milk in a food processor and blend well. Blend in squash, margarine, sugar and orange peel. In a bowl, combine flour, baking powder and salt. Pour blended ingredients from processor into dry ingredients and mix well. Stir in raisins. Fill lightly-greased or paper-lined muffin cups 3/4 full. Bake at 375° for 20-25 minutes.

Makes 12 muffins.

Acorn Squash Muffins

2 1/2 cups ALL-PURPOSE FLOUR
2 tsp. BAKING POWDER
1/2 tsp. BAKING SODA
1/2 tsp. SALT
2 EGGS, lightly beaten

1 cup cooked and mashed
   ACORN SQUASH
1 Tbsp. BUTTER
1 cup SUGAR

Preheat oven to 400°. Grease or line a 12 cup muffin tin. Combine flour, baking powder, baking soda and salt in a large mixing bowl and mix. Add eggs, squash, butter and sugar and beat until mixed. Batter should be lumpy. Fill cups to 3/4 full and bake 15 minutes or until muffins test done. Serve warm.

Zucchini Muffins

3 cups ALL-PURPOSE FLOUR
1 tsp. BAKING POWDER
1 tsp. BAKING SODA
1/2 tsp. SALT
1 tsp. CINNAMON
1 cup SUGAR

4 EGGS, room temperature
1 cup OIL
2 cups grated, ZUCCHINI
1 tsp. VANILLA
1 cup chopped WALNUTS
1/2 cup GOLDEN RAISINS

In a bowl, sift together flour, baking powder, baking soda, salt and cinnamon; set aside. In a mixing bowl, combine sugar and eggs and beat with electric mixer on Medium for 2 minutes. Gradually add oil in a slow, steady stream, beating constantly for 2-3 minutes. Add zucchini and vanilla and blend well. Stir in walnuts and raisins. Add flour mixture and stir just until batter is evenly moistened; do not overmix. Spoon into greased muffin cups. Bake at 375° for 20 minutes. Cool in pan for 10 minutes, then turn out onto wire rack.

Makes 24 muffins.

Zucchini Cake

3 cups grated ZUCCHINI
1 1/2 cups VEGETABLE OIL
3 cups SUGAR
4 EGGS
2 tsp. VANILLA
3 cups FLOUR

1 1/2 tsp. BAKING SODA
1 1/2 tsp. BAKING POWDER
1 1/2 tsp. CINNAMON
1 cup RAISINS
1 cup chopped WALNUTS

In a mixing bowl, combine zucchini, oil, sugar, eggs and vanilla and mix well. In a separate bowl, mix together remaining ingredients. Add dry ingredients to zucchini mixture and mix well. Pour into a 13 x 9 baking pan. Bake at 350° for 1 hour.

Chocolate Zucchini Cake

1/2 cup BUTTER, softened
1/2 cup VEGETABLE OIL
1 3/4 cups SUGAR
3 EGGS
2 1/2 cups FLOUR
1/4 cup COCOA
1/2 cup SOUR MILK
1 tsp. BAKING SODA
1/2 tsp. BAKING POWDER

1/2 tsp. SALT
1/2 tsp. CINNAMON
1 tsp. VANILLA
2 cups shredded ZUCCHINI
1/4 cup BROWN SUGAR
1/4 cup chopped WALNUTS
1/2 cup SEMI-SWEET
    CHOCOLATE CHIPS

In a large bowl, combine butter and oil. Add sugar and eggs and cream mixture until smooth. Beat in flour, cocoa and sour milk. Add baking soda, baking powder, salt, cinnamon and vanilla and mix well. Stir in zucchini. Pour batter into a greased 13 x 9 baking pan. In a small bowl, combine brown sugar, walnuts and chocolate chips. Sprinkle mixture on top of batter. Bake at 350° for 40 minutes. Cool in pan on rack.

Note: To make sour milk, add 1 tsp. vinegar to 1/2 cup milk.

Zucchini Pie

4 cups peeled, sliced ZUCCHINI
1 cup WARM WATER
1/2 cup SUGAR
1 cup packed BROWN SUGAR

1 tsp. CINNAMON
1 tsp. CREAM OF TARTAR
1 (9-inch) unbaked PIE
  SHELL

In a saucepan, cook zucchini in salted water until tender; drain well. Place zucchini in a bowl; add warm water, white and brown sugars, cinnamon and cream of tartar and mix well. Pour mixture into pie shell. Bake at 350° for 20 minutes or until set and golden brown. Remove from oven and cool.

Delicious Pumpkin-Pecan Pie

3 3/4 cups chopped fresh PUMPKIN
1 can (14 oz.) SWEETENED CONDENSED MILK
2 EGGS
1 tsp. CINNAMON
1/2 tsp. NUTMEG
1/2 tsp. GINGER
1/2 tsp. SALT
1 unbaked 9-inch PIE SHELL
1/2 cup PECAN HALVES
3 Tbsp. DARK BROWN SUGAR
3 Tbsp. WHIPPING CREAM

Combine pumpkin, milk, eggs and seasonings in a processor bowl. Pulse just until blended. Pour pumpkin mixture into pie shell and bake at 375° for 50-55 minutes or until knife inserted halfway between center and edge of pie comes out clean. Cool slightly. Sprinkle pecans around outer edge of pie. Combine sugar and whipping cream in a small saucepan; cook over medium heat, stirring constantly until sugar dissolves. Reduce heat and simmer 5 minutes; let cool 5 minutes. Spoon over pecans.

Zucchini Marmalade

5 cups peeled, shredded ZUCCHINI
1 can (20 oz.) CRUSHED
    PINEAPPLE, with juice
3/4 cup LEMON JUICE
3/4 cup ORANGE JUICE
4 cups SUGAR
1/4 cup MARASCHINO
    CHERRIES
1 pkg. (3 oz.) ORANGE
    JELL-O®

In a large bowl, combine zucchini, pineapple with juice, lemon juice, orange juice and sugar. Mix well; cover and refrigerate overnight. In a saucepan, combine zucchini mixture and cherries; cook for 35 minutes, stirring frequently. When mixture begins to thicken, add Jell-O and stir until dissolved. Spoon into 6 sterilized jelly jars and seal according to manufacturer's directions.

Orange-Zucchini Jam

5-6 ZUCCHINI, peeled, seeded and grated
1 3/4 cups SUGAR
1 can (11 oz.) MANDARIN ORANGES, reserve 1/2 of juice
1 pkg. (3 oz.) ORANGE JELL-O®

In a large saucepan, add zucchini and enough water to cover. Boil for 10 minutes; drain. Stir in sugar, oranges and reserved juice. Boil for an additional 10 minutes. Remove pan from heat and stir in Jell-O. Mix well. Pour mixture into sterilized jars and seal according to manufacturer's instructions.

Imitation Peach Jam

6 cups shredded ZUCCHINI
6 cups SUGAR
1 can (20 oz.) CRUSHED
    PINEAPPLE, with juice
1/2 cup LEMON JUICE
1 pkg. (1.75 oz.) SURE-JELL®
2 pkgs. (3 oz. ea.) PEACH
    GELATIN

In a large saucepan, combine the first 4 ingredients and boil for 25 minutes; add Sure-Jell. Boil for an additional 25 minutes. Stir in peach gelatin and boil for 5 minutes. Pour into sterilized jelly glasses and seal according to manufacturer's directions.

Index

More Cook Books from Golden West Publishers

TOO MANY CHILES!

75 tasty chile recipes for your table and growing and preserving techniques too! This handy reference covers virtually everything that can be done with fresh chiles. Includes recipes for chile vinegars and oils as well as fiery ketchup, mustard, jelly and butters! By Dave DeWitt and Nancy Gerlach.

5 1/2 x 8 1/2—104 pages . . . $7.95

CORN LOVERS COOK BOOK

Over 100 delicious recipes! Try *Corn Chowder, Corn Soufflé, Apple Cornbread* or *Caramel Corn,* to name a few. You will find a tempting recipe for every occasion in this collection. Includes corn facts and trivia too!

5 1/2 x 8 1/2 — 88 pages . . . $6.95

BEAN LOVERS COOK BOOK

Recipes featuring beans, lentils and legumes. Provides endless combinations for appetizers, main dishes, soups, salads and desserts. Presents beans as fun and flavorful alternatives to meat and poultry. Also includes tips for soaking, cooking and preparing beans.

5 1/2 x 8 1/2 — 112 Pages . . . $6.95

PUMPKIN LOVERS COOK BOOK

It's pumpkin time again! More than 175 recipes for soups, breads, muffins, pies, cakes, cheesecakes, cookies, ice cream, and more! Includes pumpkin trivia!

5 1/2 x 8 1/2—128 Pages . . . $6.95

VEGGIE LOVERS COOK BOOK

Everyone will love these no-cholesterol, no-animal recipes! Over 200 nutritious, flavorful recipes by Chef Morty Star. Includes a foreword by Dr. Michael Klaper. Nutritional analysis for each recipe to help you plan a healthy diet.

5 1/2 x 8 1/2 — 128 pages . . . $6.95

BERRY LOVERS COOK BOOK

Over 120 delicious recipes featuring flavorful and nutritious berries! Try *Blueberry Buttermilk Muffins, Strawberry Peach Meringue Pie, Raspberry Dream Bars, Blackberry Summer Salad* or *Boysenberry Mint Frosty* and many more. Tempting recipes for all occasions. Includes berry facts and trivia!

5 1/2 x 8 1/2 — 96 pages . . . $6.95

APPLE LOVERS COOK BOOK

Celebrating America's favorite—the apple! 150 recipes for main and side dishes, appetizers, salads, breads, muffins, cakes, pies, desserts, beverages, and preserves, all kitchen-tested by Shirley Munson and Jo Nelson.

5 1/2 x 8 1/2 — 120 Pages . . . $6.95

TAKE THIS CHILE & STUFF IT!

Fantastic, authentic recipes for *Chiles Rellenos!* Also includes salads, side dishes and *Aguas Frescas* (Mexican fruit drinks). Try *Chiles Rellenos de Frijoles Refritos* (Chiles stuffed with refried beans), *Crab-Stuffed Baked Chiles* or *Chiles Stuffed with Squash Blossoms* and more!

5 1/2 x 8 1/2 — 88 pages . . . $6.95

RECIPES FOR A HEALTHY LIFESTYLE

Recipes for maintaining your health! Appetizing low cholesterol, low fat, low sodium, low sugar recipes by nutritionist Virginia Defendorf. Includes nutritional analysis for each recipe!

5 1/2 x 8 1/2 — 128 Pages . . . $6.95

SALSA LOVERS COOK BOOK

More than 180 taste-tempting recipes for salsas that will make every meal a special event! Salsas for salads, appetizers, main dishes and desserts! Put some salsa in your life! By Susan K. Bollin. More than 260,000 copies in print!

5 1/2 x 8 1/2—128 pages . . . $6.95

ORDER BLANK

GOLDEN WEST PUBLISHERS

☼ 4113 N. Longview Ave. • Phoenix, AZ 85014
www.goldenwestpublishers.com • **1-800-658-5830** • FAX 602-279-6901

Qty	Title	Price	Amount
	Apple Lovers Cook Book	6.95	
	Bean Lovers Cook Book	6.95	
	Berry Lovers Cook Book	6.95	
	Corn Lovers Cook Book	6.95	
	Easy Recipes for Wild Game & Fish	6.95	
	Iowa Cook Book	6.95	
	Kentucky Cook Book	6.95	
	New Mexico Cook Book	6.95	
	North Carolina Cook Book	6.95	
	Oregon Cook Book	6.95	
	Pecan Lovers Cook Book	6.95	
	Pumpkin Lovers Cook Book	6.95	
	Recipes for a Healthy Lifestyle	6.95	
	Salsa Lovers Cook Book	6.95	
	Seafood Lovers Cook Book	6.95	
	Squash Lovers Cook Book	6.95	
	Take This Chile & Stuff It!	6.95	
	Too Many Chiles Cook Book	6.95	
	Veggie Lovers Cook Book	6.95	
	Wisconsin Cook Book	6.95	

Shipping & Handling Add: United States $3.00
Canada & Mexico $5.00—All others $12.00

☐ My Check or Money Order Enclosed

☐ MasterCard ☐ VISA ($20 credit card minimum)

Total $ _____

(Payable in U.S. funds)

Acct. No. _____ Exp. Date _____

Signature _____

Name _____ Phone _____

Address _____

City/State/Zip _____

Call for a FREE catalog of all of our titles

5/03   This order blank may be photocopied   Squash Lovers